JAMES BARTHOLOMEW

THE RICHEST MAN
IN THE WORLD
The Sultan of Brunei

VIKING

VIKING

Published by the Penguin Group

27 Wrights Lane, London w8 5tz, England

Viking Penguin Inc., 40 West 23rd Street, New York, New York 10010, USA

Penguin Books Australia Ltd, Ringwood, Victoria, Australia

Penguin Books Canada Ltd, 2801 John Street, Markham, Ontario, Canada l3r 1b4

Penguin Books (NZ) Ltd, 182–190 Wairau Road, Auckland 10, New Zealand

Penguin Books Ltd, Registered Offices: Harmondsworth, Middlesex, England

First published 1989

2 4 6 8 10 9 7 5 3 1

Filmset in Monophoto Bembo

Printed in Great Britain by Richard Clay Ltd, Bungay, Suffolk

A CIP catalogue record for this book is available from the British Library

ISBN 0–670–82152–7

To my mother

Contents

_____ ◌̇ _____

List of Illustrations

—————— ❖ ——————

The Sultan of Brunei (*Reflex Picture Agency*)

The Sultan with his father, the Seri Begawan (*Straits Times, Singapore*)

Queen Saleha (*Straits Times, Singapore*)

Queen Mariam (*Alan Davidson/Alpha*)

The throne room of the Istana Nurul Iman (*Oberto Gili, Conde Nast Publications*)

Kampong Ayer (*James Bartholomew*)

Enrique Zobel (*Far Eastern Economic Review*)

Dorchester Hotel (*Keystone Collection*)

Prince Billah with Terry Griffiths (*Rex Features*)

The Aviary (*James Bartholomew*)

The Prince and Princess of Wales with Mohamed Al-Fayed (*Photographers International*)

Mohamed Al-Fayed with Dame Edna Everage (*Associated Press*)

Adnan Khashoggi, the Swami, 'Tiny' Rowland and Mamaji (*Illustrated Weekly, India*)

The Swami with the Sultan of Brunei (*Illustrated Weekly, India*)

Khoo Teck Puat (*Financial Times*)

The Sultan with Lee Kuan Yew (*Straits Times, Singapore*)

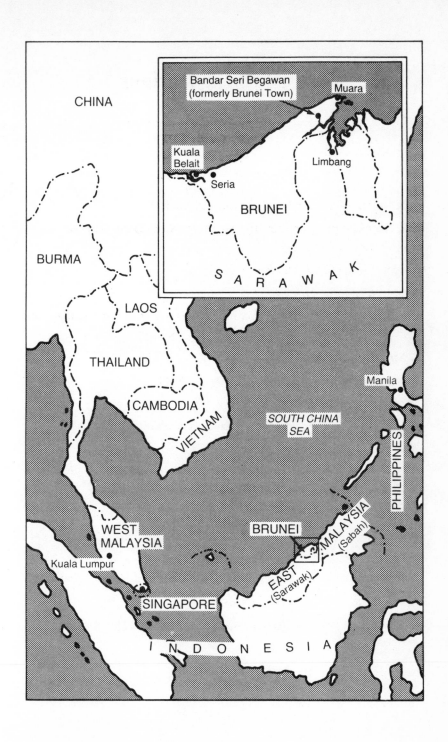

Preface

———— $\overset{\cdot\cdot}{\smile}$ ————

The Sultan does not want this book to appear. This book is not one of those flattering accounts of royalty written with the cooperation of the subject or those close to him. A firm of Washington lawyers, Williams and Connolly, have written to Viking Penguin on the Sultan's behalf, saying: 'His Majesty has in the past and continues in the present to protect his privacy and reputation.' They add: 'He has not authorized Mr Bartholmew [*sic*] to write about him and has not otherwise cooperated with Mr Bartholmew [*sic*] in any such endeavor.'

The Sultan is the absolute ruler of some 230,000 people and has kept individuals in jail without trial under 'Emergency' laws that have remained in force for a quarter of a century. His powerful public role removes, in my view, any right he might otherwise have to privacy. But his power and massive wealth make his desire for privacy a considerable obstacle to research. Those close to the Sultan know that if they are discovered talking to the media about him, they will be in trouble. They depend on him for their liveli-hood. Expatriates in Brunei also need him – for the success of their businesses. Some companies working for the Sultan have a secrecy clause written into their contracts. So, many people will either say very little or nothing at all.

Even the most willing sources have to calculate whether a par-ticular piece of information can be traced back to them. They decline to speak on the telephone from Brunei. (It is widely believed that the Brunei equivalent of the Special Branch monitors international calls.) In such circumstances, facts are not easily won and are often difficult to confirm. None the less, I have researched this book exhaustively, and am satisfied that all the facts in it are accurate.

No one wants to be quoted. One interviewee, a former member of the SAS, threatened my life if I named him in the book. More temperate souls told me at the outset of interviews that everything they said must be 'unattributable'. And in fact I have attributed almost nothing: I have wanted to protect all those people who had sufficient trust in me to tell me a part of what they know. To all these sources, unnamed for their own sakes, I say a heartfelt thank you.

CHAPTER ONE

Beyond the Dreams of Avarice

All else – valour, a good name, glory, everything in heaven and earth – is secondary to the charm of riches.

Horace *Satires*, 35–30 BC

This book is about one man's extraordinary wealth. It is about the ultimate example of personal wealth in modern times. This man is literally the richest man in the world (as *The Guinness Book of World Records* and *Fortune* magazine agree). This man's story tells us how sweet or bitter it may be to have everything money can buy. His example is the ultimate test of whether money can make you happy or whether supremely large wealth can only bring supremely large problems.

This man wanted to buy a substantial house in the English countryside, something large enough for his family, retinue and servants. He wanted somewhere peaceful, where he could relax from the usual pressures of his active life. Estate agents sent him the details of a variety of homes for him to consider. He picked one out and bought it.

On his next trip to London he decided to visit his new house. He arranged to drive out to it, following someone in another car who would lead him there. Unfortunately, the two cars became separated in traffic. Nothing daunted, the man continued on into the English countryside. The house, he knew, was in the neighbourhood of Guildford in Surrey, a comfortable 'stockbroker-belt' area. The man found Guildford but, much to his frustration, he could not find the house. He doggedly drove around Guildford for two and a half hours looking for it. In the end, he gave up.

His conclusion was that an unfindable house was not worth having. He therefore sold it.

This same man bought a house in Kensington Palace Gardens. This is a private avenue in London monitored by police at both ends. It runs alongside Kensington Palace, the home of Prince Charles, Princess Diana and Princess Margaret. Most of the large houses in this avenue are embassies (including the Soviet Embassy). No British citizen owns a house here. But this man does.

This man is so wealthy that he is spending a fortune to make this house smaller. Whereas the up-and-coming struggle for planning permission to increase the size of their buildings, this man is so rich he can knowingly reduce the value of his London mansion to make it more elegant.

His wealth gives him extraordinary freedom. It enables him not only to treat a lost house like a golf ball, but also, when he wants a weekend anywhere in the world, simply to fly there, since he has his own private fleet of aeroplanes. When he took a fancy to Impressionist art, he just came to London and bought some. Since he likes the Dorchester Hotel, he bought it. He likes polo, so he bought himself the best ponies in the world. He wanted a room always available for him in Singapore, so he bought another hotel. He took a fancy to the Beverly Hills Hotel, so he bought it. He wanted an Olympic-sized pool, so he bought one of those, too. He took up golf, and so he had an international standard golf course built outside one of his palaces. The list goes on and on. Instead of, 'What can I afford?' – the question most of us ask ourselves – he wonders, 'What do I really want?'

Supreme wealth tests his personality in a unique way. He can buy from anywhere in the world and price is not a consideration. He can buy his absolute ideal. The only problem is to decide what is the nature of his ideal. He is forced to express his personality and taste in a way that most people never have to face. He comes right up against what he wants and thus what he is. The only limit is the limit of the imagination. If he can think of it, he can have it. This can be a real challenge, but help is at hand. If he can't think of an idea, he can hire someone else to think of it.

In fact, he does not even have to hire someone: they come to him. His wealth attracts salesmen from everywhere, including the most accomplished of them in their very different guises. They include the stuffed-shirt bankers of the City of London along with Indonesian magic men, US Secretaries of State, Adnan Khashoggi, the Middle East arms dealer, an Indian guru, American investment advisors, prostitute-procurers, Mr Ten-per-cents and Mr Twenty-per-cents and the outright con-men and crooks of the world. This man has hundreds of salesmen at his door all the time and some of them are willing to spend years ingratiating themselves.

His wealth affects other people, especially those who try to take a share of it. This man has had to develop great caution in his dealings with almost everyone, since so many people are after his money. There is practically no one he can trust absolutely – too much money is at stake. A friendly word from a diplomat or a polo player or even a member of his family is never wholly above suspicion. He has so much wealth that if he took a liking to one of them he could transform their lives. His money makes him a prisoner in the mental fortress in which he must place himself for his own protection. He cannot let down the drawbridge without risk. But unless he lets others in, he remains isolated.

Some people say that their feet are so solidly on the ground that they would not be influenced by his wealth. Maybe they are right. Maybe if they met him at a party they would treat him exactly as any other person. They would not smile more than usual or find agreeable things to say. They would not find a compliment coming to their lips and would tell him, if he invited them for dinner, that they were otherwise engaged. There may be such people.

But the temptation of so much wealth is hard to resist. It is a magnet that draws all the iron filings towards it. Most people sell out even if they don't make a sale. They may deny it, but they know it in their hearts. This man knows it too. It is part of his world, part of being the richest man in the world – part of being Hassanal Bolkiah, 29th Sultan of Brunei.

CHAPTER TWO

Born in a Garden Hut

> If I had realized how rich he was going to become, I would have
> been a lot nicer to him.
>
> A former schoolmate of the Sultan, 1987

Sultan Hassanal Bolkiah, the 29th Sultan of Brunei, was born in a
garden hut. This is what his irascible late father, who carried on a
public argument with his son a few years ago, said. However, the
official brochure issued by the Ministry of Law maintains (more
predictably) that, on 15 July 1946, the Sultan was born at the Istana
Darussalam – the Darussalam palace.

Palace or hut, the richest man in the world was born into circumstances that were humble compared to his current lifestyle.
The Japanese had not long given up their wartime occupation of
Brunei, and, before leaving, had done their best to destroy the
oilfields. So the country was poor. During the Japanese occupation, the present Sultan's father, Omar Ali Saifuddien, had been
brought down by the Japanese to the level of manual labour – a
humiliation he would never forget. Omar Ali Saifuddien was not,
at that time, Sultan, but only the brother of the Sultan. Therefore
his son, Hassanal Bolkiah, was not brought up expecting to
become Sultan; he had little prospect of ever becoming Brunei's
head of state. The rise of Hassanal to the heights of being the
richest man in the world needed good luck.

But first, what and where is Brunei?

Brunei is in the Far East, in Borneo, which is the third largest
island in the world. It sits in the South China Sea, south of

mainland South-East Asia. To the east are the Philippines, to the west Indonesia.

Brunei itself is very small. It consists of only two tiny wedges hammered in to the north side of the great island. The country is covered with lush, tropical jungle – an impenetrable hotbed of trees, flowers, snakes, birds and giant insects. Until very recently, the best way to travel in Brunei was by boat on one of the rivers. There are still some tribespeople – Ibans, Muruts, Kedayans, Dayaks, Dusuns and others – who lead the life of the jungle, as their forefathers did.

Brunei takes its royalty and aristocracy very seriously, despite the fact that the country is tiny and its population of 230,000 is only half that of Edinburgh. The length of the Sultan's full name reflects the great respect he is given. Using initials for his various honours and titles, to keep it within reason, it is:

His Majesty Paduka Seri Baginda Sultan and Yang Di-Pertuan, Sultan Hassanal Bolkiah Mu'izzaddin Waddaulah Ibni Al-Marhum Sultan Haji Omar Ali Saifuddien Sa'adul Khairi Waddien, D K M B, D K, P S S U B, D P K G, D P K T, P S P N B, P S N B, P S L J, S P M B, P A N B, G C M G, D M N, D K (Kelantan), D K (Johor), D K (Negeri Sembilan), Collar of the Supreme Order of the Chrysanthemum, Grand Order of the Mugunghwa, D K (Pahang), B R I, Collar of the Nile, the Order of Al-Hussein bin Ali, the Civil Order of Oman, D K (Selangor), D K (Perlis), P G A T, Sultan and Yang Di-Pertuan Negara Brunei Darussalam.

Brunei's sense of its own importance derives, in part, from its past.

Brunei was the centre of a minor empire in the sixteenth century. It held sway over the whole of Borneo and many islands around, even including parts of the modern Philippines. Converted to Islam by missionaries from the Middle East, as Brunei developed its empire, it simultaneously made further Muslim conversions. This brought it into conflict with Spain, which had converted the Philippines to Catholicism and wanted to make Brunei Catholic too. Inevitably, the two empires had to fight it out and the ensuing river battle was overwhelmingly won by the Spanish. However, the victors then came down with cholera and had to sail away. Brunei's existence as a Muslim state thus depended entirely on a random attack of bacteria.

From the seventeenth century onwards, Brunei all but collapsed. The country was corrupt, the royal family fought among themselves and law and order broke down. Brunei became a haven for pirates. The empire self-destructed.

British colonialism intervened in its most ruthless form. The Brooke family took over a large part of what had been Brunei as its own personal fiefdom. The British government occasionally promised to restrain the rampant Brookes, but did not keep its promises.

Then, in 1903, oil was discovered. Perhaps it was not pure coincidence that two years later, in 1905, Britain took what little was left of Brunei in hand by making the country a protectorate, which it remained (apart from the period of Japanese occupation during the war) until 1984, when it achieved full independence and joined the United Nations.

Hassanal's father, Omar, became Sultan in 1953, after the death of his brother. On his death, Omar was not the next in line to the throne, but the attempt to make the legitimate heir, the daughter of the dead Sultan, into a Sultana was an embarrassing failure. And so Omar took over.

Even then, when young Hassanal had become heir to the throne, though his lifestyle was privileged by local standards, in no way was it grand or luxurious, as it is now. Brunei's wealth was only gradually being rebuilt. The so-called capital, then known as Brunei Town, was like a village – a rather bare-looking village, far from the centres of civilization as it baked in the tropical sun.

Prince Hassanal lived in a house that was called a palace, but it bore no resemblance to the two huge palaces in which he now resides. The palace of his youth was at the edge of Kampong Ayer, a traditional Brunei water-village adjacent to the centre of the capital where the houses were supported on stilts. Little had changed since the sixteenth century. When Magellan's fleet on the first circumnavigation of the world visited Brunei in 1521, the capital of Brunei was one large water-village.

Hassanal's father, Sultan Omar, was strong-willed but carried his royal position with modesty. He could often be seen walking around the town like any other man: he would say hallo to the people in the street; he would go to dinner with British expatriate businessmen. He was accessible.

He was also a devout Muslim. The money he spent on his faith made a far more ostentatious show than anything he spent on himself. He built a magnificent traditional mosque with a gold-covered dome at the edge of the capital near Kampong Ayer. The mosque is named after him and still dominates the town today. Hassanal was thus brought up in an atmosphere of devout religious faith. And Brunei generally, paralleling the trend in other Muslim countries, has gradually become more fundamentalist since the war.

But as well as being a devout Muslim, Sultan Omar was also an Anglophile: he loved all things English, and his hero was Sir Winston Churchill. He even built a museum to honour the British leader, and curiously, it is the only museum in the world exclusively to commemorate Churchill. Filled with artefacts from Churchill's life, such as uniforms, books and pictures, it tells the story of his rich life, illustrated by photographs and displays. It is a bizarre feeling when visiting Brunei to withdraw from the tropical heat and the open drains to listen to Churchill's voice making rousing speeches during the London blitz.

Sultan Omar's Anglophilia even extended to the acquisition of a traditional London taxi. Hassanal Bolkiah, together with his brothers and sisters, were often driven in the taxi to watch films in one of the cinemas in the capital.

As with many father–son relationships, Hassanal both accepted and rejected his father's guidance. He would rebel against much of what his father taught him, but he also accepted much of it, probably far more than he realized. In loving and at other times in fighting his father, in accepting some of his attitudes and in opposing others, the son was formed by the father.

Sultan Omar's most influential characteristic – that which most affected his son Hassanal – was his dominating personality. Sultan Omar was generally feared and respected. He benefited from a still-lingering belief among Bruneians that their Sultan should be

7

revered, and this respect verged on the belief that the Sultan was sacred. Since Sultan Omar was also a determined, wily man it is small wonder that his young son should find him awesome.

This is probably part of the reason why young Hassanal became so shy. He may also have taken to heart the fact that his father preferred Hassanal's older sister, Masna, to his eldest son. In any event, Hassanal's early years made him quiet and introverted.

Hassanal's early education was in the palace. He had a private tutor from Malaya named Dato Ghani, who is alive today and lives in what has now become Malaysia. Much of Hassanal's education came from Malay teachers: the dominant race in Brunei is of Malay origin and speaks a version of the Malay language.

Hassanal's private education did not bring the boy out of himself. Not until he was fourteen, in 1961, did Hassanal leave the closed world of the palace in Brunei to go to regular schools. He studied at the Jalan Gurney School and subsequently at the Victorian Institution, both in Kuala Lumpur, the capital of Malaysia.

The Victorian Institution was a typical British colonial public school, attended by the elite of Malaysia. The building was and is very grand, standing on a slight rise overlooking an expanse of playing fields. The school espoused the old British public-school traditions of sport and discipline. The Victorian Institution was an advertisement for British colonialism. And it must have been quite a shock for Hassanal Bolkiah.

He was not up to it: he was neither bright enough nor confident enough. Although he studied at the school from 1962 to 1964, when he was aged between fifteen and seventeen, the school newspaper reported later that he attended Forms One, Two and Three. But children attending these forms are usually aged between twelve and fifteen. In other words he attended classes for children who were two years younger than he. Hassanal was in the same form as his brother, Mohamed, who was also two years younger than Hassanal. But even with this two-year advantage over his classmates, Hassanal was still a poor student. A classmate remembers Hassanal was 'a bit of a dud', whereas his brother Mohamed was 'much more intelligent'.

The teachers at the Victorian Institution were trained to show no special respect to the children of VIPs, as part of Britain's public-school ethic. In any case, there were plenty of other children of VIPs in the school, so no one paid particular attention to Hassanal. 'If I had realized how rich he was going to become, I would have been a lot nicer to him,' says one of his contemporaries. One teacher, Valentine Manuel, certainly paid no exaggerated respect to his royal pupil. 'You are a dud!' he used to exclaim. 'You don't deserve to be in my class! Get out!' Hassanal was not the only boy to be thrown out of the classroom. It was normal practice when boys failed to answer questions. But Hassanal got more than his fair share of expulsions with the words, 'You are a dud!' ringing in his ears. Hassanal was shy and quiet when he arrived; this treatment could only make his condition worse. Even the school newspaper describes him as 'quiet'. A classmate says he was 'very reserved . . . he didn't speak out'.

Hassanal was also told off by teachers when the class mis-behaved. As form monitor he was meant to be responsible for them. Sometimes the teacher would demand to know who had been responsible for a misdemeanour. But Hassanal, tight-lipped as ever and probably keeping to a boys' code of solidarity, would refuse to say anything. So he would be shouted at again and sent out again. He did not exhibit much interest in academic work and he did not complete his academic year in Form Three: he left before the exam.

He was not even a success on the sports field, which would have made him far more important in the eyes of his classmates than being the son of a Sultan. Instead Prince Hassanal, at this time, was stout. He had a 'big tummy' says a contemporary. The blows to his confidence which the Sultan received at school were dangerous. He would need all his confidence in later life to be able to refuse the false friendship of people who were after his money.

But there was one area in which Hassanal did do well and his success in this single sphere has influenced him up to the pre-sent. This was his great success in the Cadet Corps, where he was named the 'School's Best Cadet' in 1964. A contemporary says he was 'very disciplined'. This discipline was probably something that his father had instilled in him, in tune with Sultan Omar's great respect for military excellence. But Hassanal in later life showed a love/hate relationship with discipline. In some respects he would take it to an extreme, in others, he would leave it aside. Nevertheless, when it came to the discipline required at the Victorian Institution Cadet Corps, Hassanal excelled.

After leaving the Victorian Institution, Hassanal returned to Brunei, where he attended a school named after his father. Then, in 1965, fourteen days after his nineteenth birthday, Hassanal Bolkiah married his cousin, Princess Saleha, who is described in a flattering, privately published book about the Sultan as being at that time 'a sweet, be-dimpled, soulful-eyed lass of sixteen'. This very early marriage, only a year after Hassanal had been in classes with fifteen-year-old boys, was surely the idea of Sultan Omar. Hassanal was too young and from too controlled a background to have had wide experience of girlfriends. He was still dominated by his father, whose sense of family and royal dignity was intense. It is almost certainly the case that Sultan Omar firmly encouraged Hassanal to make this marriage. In most Western countries, marriage to such a close relative is usually frowned upon. But the marriage unified two important branches of the family springing from a previous Sultan. And this was probably Sultan Omar's intention. The unification process was taken still further, as a brother and sister of Hassanal each married a sister and brother of Princess Saleha.

Hassanal was married even before he had finished his education. In January 1966, six months after his wedding, he was sent to the Royal Military Academy at Sandhurst. As Britain's most prestigious officer-training academy, Sandhurst had the status required for the first son of a Sultan. It also reflected the success Hassanal had achieved as a cadet at the Victorian Institution. Hassanal was part of Intake 40. He was put in Ypres Company, New College. His brother Mohamed, who went to Sandhurst at the same time, was put in Rhine Company in Victory College.

During his two years at Sandhurst, Hassanal did not particularly distinguish himself. His specialization in International Affairs was Russia. His Adjutant at Sandhurst wrote, 'Probably the highest advantage he gained is having had a tough training in self-discipline and responsibility, the most important factors in his future life.'

His 'future life' was coming faster than anyone thought.

Ever since the war, Brunei had been moving towards democracy. It seemed likely that Brunei would be part of the major post-war moves towards independence, towards new, large countries made out of small states, towards democracy and perhaps even towards Communism. But Sultan Omar was the de Gaulle of Brunei. He was stubborn, astute and brave enough to stand against forces that seemed invincible. He successfully held out against all the trends of his time and managed to make Brunei the non-Communist, non-democratic Sultanate that it is today. Without Sultan Omar's successes his son Hassanal would not now be Sultan. Hassanal was lucky in his choice of father.

Sultan Omar even held out for a long time against independence from Britain. He valued Britain's military protection which proved particularly valuable in 1962 when Sultan Omar faced an armed revolt. The revolt came about because the Sultan persistently postponed the first Legislative Council meeting to include democratically elected representatives.

Sultan Omar called on the British, who sent over crack Gurkha troops and quickly crushed the amateur rebellion. But by 1967 the British government had changed its attitude; formed now by the Labour Party instead of the Conservative Party, it agreed with the voters of Brunei that democracy should be introduced. With pressure from both sides, it seemed that Sultan Omar would be forced to give in.

Sultan Omar's answer to this powerful pressure was both original and successful. He abdicated. In haste, young Prince Hassanal was recalled from England. He missed the Sandhurst Sovereign's Parade (taken on 14 December by Admiral Sir Varyl Begg, First Sea Lord). He was rushed back to Brunei against his own will. According to one account, 'he practically had to be abducted'. The ceremony took place on 5 October 1967. For Hassanal it was reportedly 'bittersweet and confusing'. He was still only twenty-one.

Hassanal's rapid progress from schoolboy failure to head of state was a frightening experience for him. But in fact his father continued to make the decisions. The only change was that if the British wanted to press a point the Seri Begawan (Sultan Omar's new title) could now say, 'Don't speak to me, speak to my son. He is the Sultan!' Sultan Hassanal Bolkiah began his reign an unselfconfident puppet of his father and he remained a puppet for the next fifteen years or so. When the British Resident, as the representative of the British government, had an audience with the young Sultan, the Seri Begawan would always be there. The young Sultan said little, remaining as shy and reserved as he had been at school.

Thus began the reign of the present Sultan. His sudden elevation was literally the *coup de grâce* of his father's reign. Hassanal had, by virtue of political expediency, become the Sultan of Brunei, but that still did not make him extraordinarily rich. He needed more good luck to become abundantly wealthy. And he got it.

CHAPTER THREE

Money! Money! Money!

——————— ॐ ———————

I smell oil!

The Hon. T. G. Cochrane, Brunei, 1926

Even before oil was first discovered in Brunei in 1903, in the nine-teenth century British colonialists had complained of 'brackish' water in the marshes, which in part reflected the fact that Brunei was liter-ally oozing with hydrocarbons. A forerunner of the multinational, Royal Dutch/Shell started investigating Brunei's oil potential in 1909. But for a long time Shell and other companies could not find commercially viable reserves. The other companies gave up; Shell doggedly kept on searching until a crucial incident in 1926.

Two employees of Shell, a Mr F. F. Marriott and the Hon. T. G. Cochrane, were in a remote part of Brunei called Kuala Belait, which at that time consisted of a few fishermen's huts. They had borrowed a couple of old bicycles and used them to pedal along the coastline towards the camp of a Swiss geo-physicist Cochrane wanted to see. Ploughing through sand in the tropical heat, the bicycle journey was very tiring. They came to a stream called Sungei Seria and, exhausted, they lay down on the beach for a rest.

Suddenly Cochrane sat up and said, 'I smell oil!'

He subsequently persuaded Shell to search the area, which is how the first major oilfield, the 'Seria' oilfield, came to be discovered in 1929.[1] This oilfield was the beginning of Brunei's energy riches.

---

[1] *The Discovery and Development of the Seria Oilfield* by G. C. Harper, published by Muzium Brunei, 1975.

The 1929 discovery had been followed by another important one in 1963, but when Hassanal Bolkiah nervously came to the throne in 1967, these finds represented financial well-being, not fantastic wealth. At that time the price for oil was much lower than it is now – only about US$1.33 a barrel. Also, Shell took a higher percentage of what profit there was. More important still, exploitation of natural gas, which now produces more income than the oil does, had not even begun. Only in the 1970s did Brunei hit the jackpot – a double jackpot.

The first part of the jackpot was the extraordinary rise in the price of energy in that decade. In the early 1970s oil prices multiplied nine times. From only US$1.21 a barrel in 1970, the price jumped to US$10.98 in 1974.[2]

At the turn of the decade came another leap in the value of oil and gas. The price of oil trebled again, reaching an average of US $36.01 in 1980 – thirty times the price of only a decade before. Even allowing for inflation, which was rampant, the price of oil had multiplied fourteen times.

This could not have been better timed for Brunei, because the second jackpot was a tremendous increase in Brunei's energy production in the very same decade.

New discoveries meant that oil output increased from 138,000 barrels per day in 1970 to 241,000 ten years later. Since then production has been allowed to ease back again to only 165 million barrels of crude oil per day in 1986, which was deliberately well below that of which Brunei is capable. Brunei is certainly not running out of oil. The Sultan is so wealthy that he has no need to hurry production along. He can leave the oil in the ground, like money in the bank. This is partly because he is making so much money from gas.

Gas was discovered by Shell in 1963, before the technology to exploit it had been fully developed. Only in 1969 were firm development plans made, and it was not until 1973 that large-scale deliveries were made. Thus gas production arrived just in time for the best prices for energy for over a century.

[2] Average annual prices supplied by British Petroleum.

It is the gas that has made the Sultan so very wealthy. The offshore fields now yield 841 million cubic feet of gas per day. The Liquefied Natural Gas plant built to process it was, at the time of building, the biggest in the world.

Since the nearest major market for gas is Japan, one of the partners in the exploitation is Mitsubishi, which takes responsibility for marketing the gas in its home country. The gas is liquefied and shipped in tankers to Tokyo, where it ends up as gas and electricity, warming thousands of homes and boiling millions of saucepans of rice.

The Brunei government itself became a partner in the gas exploitation, reflecting the increasing power of the government to demand a higher proportion of the profits. Brunei's share of the gas profits continues to increase. In 1986 Brunei increased its equity in the transport operation (the seven tankers that commute to Tokyo Bay loaded with liquefied gas) up to 50 per cent. Brunei takes royalties and taxes on top of that.

Brunei's double jackpot – the higher energy prices combined with higher production – meant that in the course of the ten years from 1970 to 1980, the hydrocarbon-based income of Brunei rocketed. Oil and gas exports were worth Brunei $277 million in 1970. Ten years later they had soared thirty-five times, to B$9.714 million (U S$4.8 billion at the current exchange rate).

As the value of Brunei's oil and gas exports soared, there was heavy investment in new equipment, especially the equipment for exploiting the new gas field. But otherwise the costs of producing Brunei's energy only rose gently with inflation. So most of the extra income was pure profit. Since then, there have been gyrations in the income received according to the movements in energy prices, but the value of the energy sales has continued to provide massive excess income for Brunei and the Sultan. The excess is controlled by the Sultan and thus has his wealth developed into the greatest fortune in the world.

Even the setback in oil prices in 1983–6 had a silver lining. The reserves that had piled up in the boom years had been invested worldwide. When the price of oil went down, stock-markets went up. Brunei's financial reserves soared.

Calculations based on Brunei government publications and information from well-placed sources indicate that the total wealth controlled by the Sultan amounts now to more than U S$27 billion. That includes the Sultan's directly owned assets and the financial assets which are nominally owned by the Government. The Sultan himself denies he is the richest man in the world. He maintains that Brunei's reserves are quite separate from his own wealth. But the Sultan controls Brunei's reserves, just as he controls everything else in Brunei.

Hassanal Bolkiah is not only Sultan, he is also Prime Minister and Minister of Defence. One of his brothers is Minister of Finance and another is Minister of Foreign Affairs. Government is a family business in Brunei. Meanwhile, two of his most trusted helpers are respectively Deputy Minister of Defence (and therefore in authority over the armed forces) and 'Special Adviser' (the most senior of the non-royal ministers). Additionally, the State of Emergency that was declared at the time of the revolt in 1962 remains in force, giving the Sultan extended legal powers. Not only were some people imprisoned without trial during the rebellion and have been kept in jail for a quarter of a century, but more people appear to have been imprisoned without trial since 1984 (of which more in Chapter 13, 'A Devil of a State'). You challenge the Sultan at your peril.

Brunei is a private country run like a private possession. One is entitled to ask if the Sultan does not control the country's reserves, who on earth does?

The line between his personal wealth and that of the state is far from clear. It is a fact, for example, that the Sultan's bills at the Dorchester Hotel are sent to the Brunei High Commissioner in London for payment. It is also a fact that state funds were used in the building of the Istana Nurul Iman, the outsize palace which the Sultan built between 1982 and 1984. True, some of the palace is used for government operations, but there is no disclosure of where the line is drawn. Little evidence is made available of any line being drawn at all.

Two leading arbiters of what is superlative in the world – *The Guinness Book of World Records* and *Fortune* magazine – have decided to ignore the Sultan's claim to be distanced from the government's reserves. They both name him the richest man in the world. *Fortune* magazine in October 1987 calculated that his assets were US$25 billion.

The Sultan's annual income alone is greater than the total assets of all but the very richest people on earth. Only thirty-six people listed by *Fortune* are shown to have net assets above US$2 billion, which is calculated to be the Sultan's haul each and every year, free of tax. That is an income equivalent to US$5.5 million a day or US$229,000 per hour; even during his sleep he is earning US$3,819 per minute, or US$63 per second.

Of course, the Sultan's exact income and assets are secret. But they can be tracked down, starting with the latest development plan of Brunei. This includes a table showing government revenue and expenditure (the definite figures only go up to 1984, but there are 'Treasury estimates' for 1985). These estimates show total government revenue of B$4.55 billion (equivalent to US$2.2 billion).

Much of this government income is absorbed in genuine state expenditure on such things as free education, free health care and subsidized housing. But in 1985, US$935 million was expected to be left over for the Sultan to dispose of as he thought fit. That is the starting point.

Next comes income from government investments. This income is entirely excluded from the development plan. Perhaps the Sultan would prefer his subjects to forget the existence of the investments. Informed sources suggest that the reserves amounted to US$14.3 billion at the end of 1984. Taking an interest rate of 7 per cent, the income from those reserves should amount to US$1 billion a year.

In addition, there are a few other smaller items going directly to the Sultan. He receives a royalty from the oil production (the word 'royalty' never being more appropriate) which, according to industry sources, is probably at least 2 per cent of the government oil and gas revenues. He would also receive a salary for his posts as Prime Minister and Defence Minister; but that is chicken-feed. Then he has the income from his own private investments. If we assume his private investments are at least US$1 billion, then the income is probably at least US$50 million. The grand total of all his sources of income thus reaches just over US$2 billion.

The Richest Man in the World

	US Dollars (millions)
Government surplus revenue	935
Government investment income	1,000
Oil and gas royalties	25
Personal investment income	50
Total	2,010

THE SULTAN'S ASSETS

	US Dollars (billions)
Reserves at end 1984	14.3
Surplus revenue 1985	0.9
Surplus revenue 1986	0.4
Surplus revenue 1987	0.6
Investment income on reserves 1985	1.0
Investment income on reserves 1986	1.0
Investment income on reserves 1987	1.0
Currency and stock-market gains on reserves	5.7
Personal investments	1.0
Currency and stock-market gains on investments	0.4
Chattels	1.5
Total assets at the Sultan's disposal	27.8

As for his assets, the figure to start with is the reserves of US$14.3 billion in 1984. To this must be added the forecast government surplus in 1985 of US$0.9 billion and guessed government surpluses for 1986 and 1987. On top of that comes the investment income for 1985, 1986 and 1987 of US$1 billion each year. We are assuming here that the Sultan did not spend this money but spent only his direct and personal income.

The stock-markets of the world all boomed in 1985–6 and it would be surprising if Brunei's reserves and investment had not risen by 30 per cent at the very least, especially since a good proportion was invested in yen. That means a profit of US$5.7 billion.

Then there are the Sultan's investments held directly by him. If these were US$1 billion or more in 1984, he will have also made stock-market and currency gains of at least US$0.4 billion. The

Sultan's non-investment assets like palaces (the first palace alone cost U S$400 million), houses, hotels, Impressionist paintings, *objets d'art*, aeroplanes and so forth must be worth at least U S$1.5 billion.

Put everything together and the grand total for assets comes to U S$27.8 billion.

If one added in a capital value for Brunei's oil and gas reserves still in the ground, this would make the figure jump much higher. Since the oil and gas yielded a net U S$0.9 billion surplus to requirements in 1985, the net worth of these reserves to the Sultan (even after allowing for government expenditure) is some U S$15 billion (using a 6 per cent yield). But we will leave that out. We will also leave out the value of the benefits which the Sultan derives from government expenditure. That leaves the figure of U S$27.8 billion. *Fortune* estimates his wealth at 'only' U S$25 billion.

Even using this conservative U S$25 billion, the Sultan is in a different league to the rest of the world. The only other man in the game is King Fahd of Saudi Arabia, whose fortune was estimated by *Fortune* at U S$18 billion. The rest are in the second division, since all of them have wealth half or less that of the Sultan. *Fortune* estimates the wealth of the Mars family at US$12.5 million. But that is divided up among various family members. Queen Elizabeth is estimated to be worth U S$8.7 billion. Kenneth Thomson, majority owner of the International Thomson Organization, is put at U S$6 billion. He is shown as the ninth richest. By the time one reaches the eleventh richest, the wealth involved is only 20 per cent of that controlled by the Sultan. People like Sheik Jaber Al-Sabah of Kuwait, Queen Beatrix of the Netherlands, Li Ka Shing (the most successful businessman in Hongkong), Alfred Taubman (the property developer who controls Sotheby's, the auction house), Rupert Murdoch (the newspaper tycoon) and Konosuke Matsushita (who started up the Japanese electrical giant of the same name) are among the also-rans. Rupert Murdoch only has U S$1.4 billion.

The Sultan's wealth of U S$25 billion is hard to imagine. It is more than the total foreign-exchange reserves of Australia, India and South Korea put together. It would buy sufficient Rolls-Royce motor-cars that, placed end to end, they would reach across the United States, from New York to Los Angeles. Alternatively, if placed along the journey of the Orient Express train, they would reach all the way from London to Istanbul with 106,719 Rolls-Royces left over. If the US$25 billion were used to buy Moët et Chandon champagne, then the bottles, placed end to end, would reach to the moon and back with enough left over to circle the earth three times.

An averagely well-paid worker in an advanced country earning US$20,000 a year (or £11,500) would need to work 1.25 million years to earn as much – assuming he paid no tax and spent nothing for the entire period. If he was unlucky enough to be taxed and so self-indulgent as to eat and drink, saving only 10 per cent of his income, then it would take him 12.5 million years to amass the Sultan's fortune.

The Sultan's US$25 billion is bigger than the stock-market valuation of General Motors (316 million shares outstanding, priced at US$68 apiece). The US$25 billion is also bigger than the combined stock-market valuations of ICI, Jaguar and National Westminster Bank.

It is difficult to grasp. But of course lots of people try: management of this huge sum is a much coveted job. It used to be mostly in the hands of the British government, managed by an anachronistic British government agency called the Crown Agents. This was a hangover from colonial days. In 1978, Morgan Grenfell, the British merchant bank, and James Capel, the British stockbrokers, were each given a slice of the cake as a 'competitive check' on the performance of the Crown Agents. Very soon other international banks and stockbrokers started sending emissaries to try to get further slices. Wardley, the merchant-bank subsidiary of the Hongkong Bank, soon got one.

Douglas Hardy, an emissary for Citibank, was celebrated for out-Britishing the British in Brunei. He would wear suit and tie to even informal functions, regardless of the tropical heat; this showed respect to Brunei and the royal family. Hardy's hardiness eventually paid off in July 1983, when the Crown Agents were finally sacked and Citibank was one of the lucky ones to receive a management contract. Also included in the party were Morgan Guaranty and two of the four leading Japanese securities houses, Nomura and Daiwa.

The reason for the dismissal of the Crown Agents has never been authoritatively explained. It is said that it was a result of an argument between Britain and Brunei over which country should have command over the British Gurkhas. The Gurkhas have long been stationed in Brunei, after playing the leading role in saving the Sultanate from the 1962 revolt. But sources close to the British side of the negotiations deny that the dismissal of the Crown Agents was anything to do with the Gurkha issue.

Also mysterious is the reason why Wardley was sacked as one of the fund managers in 1984. There were several ingenious theories and delightful rumours, mostly centring on some offence that the Hongkong Bank parent was thought to have given to the royal family. But none can be confirmed. Wardley's place in the fund-management team was taken by the Union Bank of Switzerland.

In 1987 James Capel was also sacked. That was after James Capel became, like Wardley, a subsidiary of the Hongkong Bank. Clearly for fund managers being owned by the Hongkong Bank had become a kiss of death. The irony is that the Hongkong Bank is the biggest and probably the best commercial bank in Brunei. The bulk of the money removed from the care of James Capel was put in the hands of Baring Brothers, a respected British merchant bank.

The changing team of illustrious international fund managers has been supervised, since the sacking of the Crown Agents, by a new institution called the Brunei Investment Agency, which also manages some of the money itself. The idea is that young graduates from Brunei should learn the business of investment management from the illustrious institutions and then do more and more of it themselves.

Thus has Brunei become a hirer and firer of the world's most famous financial institutions. From being a colonial blip on the map, Brunei has become one of the most sought-after clients in the world. Even David Rockefeller of Chase Manhattan has been known to drop in for a friendly chat. Suddenly Brunei has found it has a lot more friends. And so has the Sultan.

CHAPTER FOUR

The Tree of Knowledge

——————— ِ ———————

Everything I have is for sale – at a profit.

> Adnan Khashoggi, 1987

From his accession to the throne in 1967 to the middle of the 1970s, Sultan Hassanal Bolkiah remained shy and in the shadow of his father. But during the mid 1970s, as he approached thirty and his wealth increased, he began to assert his right to do as he wished.

He could not rule. That was still his father's prerogative. He was like Edward Prince of Wales, the son of Queen Victoria. He had money, prestige and a young man's energies, but he carried no responsibilities. If he could not wield power then he had to channel his wealth and energy elsewhere. Like Prince Edward, later King Edward VII, he became a playboy. Just as Prince Edward bought himself all sorts of luxuries and ate and drank and went out, so did the Sultan. And just as Prince Edward had Lillie Langtry and other female friends, so did the young Hassanal Bolkiah.

Hassanal, though, was less well prepared than Prince Edward to walk across the quicksands of self-indulgence. Whereas Prince Edward had been self-confident and wise to the world, the young Sultan had lived in a very protected environment. The Far Eastern, Muslim backwater of Brunei was no preparation for the fleshpots of Europe.

So when he came to London in the second half of the 1970s, he took to self-indulgence like a thirsty man finding water in the desert. He drank too fast. Thrilled to discover what his money could buy, he gulped it down, encouraged all the while by the merchants of pleasure. He was fleeced. He made mistakes. He wanted to go from knowing nothing to knowing everything in one move.

Among the people delighted to find this extremely wealthy, active young man trying to catch up on life's experiences was a man equally experienced in the ways of the world as Sultan Hassanal was innocent. Adnan Khashoggi was an arms dealer in the Middle East at a time when frequent wars made successful arms dealers very rich. He ingratiated himself with some of the wealthy Arab leaders who were buying arms, and he obtained for them whatever guns, planes and missiles they wanted. His connection with the Saudi royal family was particularly valuable. But he would make any deal for anyone if it was big enough. Khashoggi was and remains the archetypal fixer.

He started fixing deals while still at college in the United States. He went on to become a master at gaining the confidence of powerful men. He made a point of appearing as rich as possible himself. He would host lavish parties and give presents even to those much wealthier than himself. Young women would be available for the pleasure of men whose friendship and goodwill he sought.

Khashoggi was at the centre of the spaghetti bowl of international connections. He was well known to the Arab leaders of the Middle East, high society in Europe and rival fixers and entrepreneurs around the globe. He was sophisticated and cunning. The Sultan fell for his urbane charm and for his vision of the good life.

Khashoggi was one of the men who introduced the Sultan to the night-club scenes of London and Paris. The Sultan's huge wealth meant that he was welcomed into London's night-club world at the highest levels. The club-owners and pleasure-seekers were keen to be his friends.

One of many places the Sultan visited was the Belfry Club in West Halkin Street, Knightsbridge, near Harrods. The Belfry, originally a church, had been converted into a dining club with private rooms upstairs that could be hired. The style was that of relaxed country elegance with plenty of light natural wood and mellow colours. Some members of the British royal family went there from time to time. So did people from the pop-music world and publishing. And so did some of the hard-core night-clubbers. Victor Lownes, the former head of Playboy's operations in Europe, was once at a cocktail party at the Belfry when he was introduced to the Sultan, who was reclining on a couch. Khashoggi had invited the Sultan to a dinner there.

Adnan Khashoggi was a friend of the operator of the Belfry – Charles Riachy. Riachy, a Lebanese Christian and a wealthy man in his own right, was a helper of Khashoggi. He was 'the fixer's fixer'. While Khashoggi got all the publicity, Riachy kept out of the limelight. But some of his background reveals the sort of world in which the Sultan, a Muslim from a water-village in Borneo, suddenly found himself.

Riachy was one of the first of the Arabs to go to London after the sudden rise in wealth of the oil-rich countries. He was an early starter in the business of arranging things for the new rich. He would suggest houses they might buy or businesses. He would cater to their needs and, no doubt, accept commissions when appropriate.

Among other roles, Riachy was a nominal shareholder in the Belfry, a British company predominantly owned by a Panamanian company, BCL Investments SA, which financially supported the club. According to the British accounts to March 1985 (the latest period available in September 1986), the club made a loss each year. The reason the Panamanian company should be willing for its subsidiary to run up an accumulated loss of £1.2 million (as at March 1985) is not at all clear.

Riachy knew his way around the clubs of London, including the casinos. He says he was employed then as a consultant to the Ladbroke Group, which was one of the major casino operators at that time. He explains that visiting casinos was fashionable and he would go to them with friends who had come from abroad. Riachy had many Arab friends and in his offices he has pictures of King Fahd and the late President Sadat. Riachy says that he would receive five telephone calls a day from different casinos trying to persuade him to visit them.

The world of London's casinos at that time was not a haven for organized crime, as in other parts of the world, but in the late 1970s and early 1980s, it was sufficiently murky for the police and the Gaming Board to decide to clean it up. In 1979, the police and the Gaming Board (joined by the Playboy Club) succeeded in bringing down the Ladbroke Group casino empire which, according to the British courts, was 'unfit' to hold a casino gaming licence. Among the allegations mentioned in court were hiring a prostitute and bribing policemen, both to obtain information. Next Corals, another major casino group, had its licences challenged for improper practices, as did Playboy. Three of the four biggest casino operators were thus thrown out of business within a few years.

One of the practices for which Ladbroke was criticized in 1979 was paying commissions to people who brought in rich gamblers to their clubs. Ladbroke did not deny the practice. The company maintained that it was common practice throughout the 'industry' and that it had not been told the practice was disapproved of by the Gaming Board until an earlier hearing that same year.

Both Khashoggi and his friend Riachy were mentioned at hearings concerning Ladbroke. There was one instance quoted in court of Riachy receiving a payment from Ladbroke (for purposes unspecified) of £19,275. Another instance was quoted of 'R' receiving £50,000. It was suggested in court that this was also Riachy. An article from the satirical magazine *Private Eye* was read in court, in which it was claimed that Riachy had received 5 per cent of the losses made by Adnan Khashoggi. The total losses Khashoggi was said, in the article, to have made were £7 million in 1975–6. However, Riachy himself denies that he ever received commission for bringing people into casinos. He says he merely went *with* people.

The important aspect of this is not who did or did not receive commissions. The important thing is that this world of casinos, where commissions, prostitutes and bribery were commonly used to make contact with rich men and persuade them to gamble, was quite a change for a young man from a little country of water-villages.

The Sultan was sighted visiting the most prestigious casino of them all – Aspinall's. Aspinall's is a casino in a class of its own in terms of decor, service and social cachet. Located in Curzon Street in Mayfair, close to the top hotels such as the Dorchester, the

Connaught and Claridges, it was formerly Curzon House, the one-time residence of Lord Howe. It is a beautiful period house filled with antique English furniture and fine Wedgwood china especially made for the casino. The Sultan was reported to have gambled there in the summer of 1985. He lost over a million pounds.

Aspinall's was not one of those casinos closed down by the courts (though its licence application was opposed by the Gaming Board at an appeal hearing in 1981). The casino was founded and run by John Aspinall, who is unusual among club operators in that he runs his club largely in order to pay for his passion – operating a zoo. John Aspinall was an acquaintance of Riachy. But that is insignificant. In this little world of London's nightlife, everybody knew everybody. The connections weaved this way and that. They reached very high and they reached very low.

But a casino, even one with Chippendale furniture and backed, incidentally, by Sir James Goldsmith, the billionaire international tycoon, is not a place where a Muslim ('Brunei's supreme religious authority', as he has designated himself) is supposed to be sighted at all. Gambling is wholly contrary to the teachings of Islam.

The Sultan's other youthful experiments included a period when he started wearing dark glasses even indoors. He grew a beard. His brothers adopted the same fashion of whiskers and dark glasses and, with their military uniforms on, they began to look like Mexican bandits in a Western.

Then there was the Sultan's love of driving prestige European sports cars at full tilt. He would even have a road in Brunei closed at night so that he could really open the throttle and speed under the stars without constraint.

In neighbouring Singapore, the Sultan took to visiting one of its most elegant hotels, the Goodwood Park. This hotel is just near the main shopping and entertainment centre, Orchard Road. It is built along grand colonial lines, although not British colonial: formerly the Teutonia Club, the hotel was built for expatriate Germans in Singapore in 1899. The Goodwood Park was and remains owned by the banker and entrepreneur Khoo Teck Puat – a Chinese Malaysian who has also become a permanent resident of Australia. Khoo Teck Puat had close relations with the Brunei royal family and was one of only two foreigners who were allowed to set up banks in Brunei.

When the Sultan visited the Goodwood Park, he stayed in the best suite. This suite had its own private lift into the sitting room. The dining room offered a wide view of Scotts Road, and the ample study with leather-top desk had pictures of ancient Borneo. When the Sultan was staying, his own portrait would be displayed. He visited the suite so often, in fact, that it was named the 'Brunei Suite'.

The stories of the Sultan's pleasure-seeking at this time are many and various. A staff member recalls that when the Sultan stayed at Goodwood Park, some of his aides would be on the look-out for women who might interest 'the boss'.

The Sultan and his brothers had villas built with private beaches where they could have parties, as well as the parties held in the palaces which sometimes lasted through the night. Women from various parts of the world were flown in to take part. One observer was amused at how nice English girls from good families were happy to come out for these parties and would return quite content with some present, such as a solid gold necklace.

Amidst the various stories, some of which were doubtless exaggerated in the telling, was one that said the Sultan was having an affair with an air hostess who worked for Royal Brunei Airlines. The story turned out to be perfectly true. As we will see later, this particular relationship developed well beyond a youthful fling. The relationship slaked, to some extent, the Sultan's youthful thirst for experience and helped bring him to a more contented maturity. It continued far longer and went much deeper than his other relationships, to the extent of causing a serious divide in the royal family.

Meanwhile there was one other major activity that Khashoggi and others like him encouraged. This was the most natural activity for an extraordinarily rich man: to buy.

CHAPTER FIVE

How to Make a Sale to a Sultan

———————— ॐ ————————

In an ugly and unhappy world, the richest man can purchase nothing
but ugliness and unhappiness.

George Bernard Shaw, 'Maxims for Revolutionists',
Man and Superman, 1903

As the growing wealth of Brunei began to be better known. The
salesmen descended.

Making a sale to the Sultan was probably not too difficult in the
early years. But it has progressively become more tricky. The first
difficulty is gaining his attention. The Sultan is protected by a large
bureaucracy and two key local figures: Pehin Isa, his 'special adviser'
and senior minister among the non-royal members of the cabinet,
and Major-General (previously Brigadier-General) Ibnu, the
Sultan's more fun-loving, polo-playing Deputy Minister of Defence.

Even if one gets past his closest advisers, there is still further to
go. The traditional route, absurd as it may seem, is to give the
Sultan a present. It may seem upside down to give the richest man
in the world a present, but that is the norm. Those who have been
most successful in selling to the Sultan tend to be those who have
given him rather spectacular presents. Most people aim too low to
gain his attention.

At a dinner party in Brunei in 1986, a representative of Jordan
asked the assembled guests for advice on what his corporate body
might give to the Sultan. 'We can't afford to give him a car. Is there
anything a bit cheaper we could give him?' he asked plaintively.

The other guests considered the problem. One of them who had regular contact with the Sultan, remarked unhelpfully, 'Well, cars and horses are the usual thing.'

'Yes,' persisted the Jordanian, 'but those are too expensive for us. We would like to give him something, but it is difficult to know what.'

It certainly is. If anyone is 'the man who has everything', it is the Sultan.

One businessman was very pleased to have found a present that he thought was truly original and prestigious. It was a piece of polo equipment, which cannot be specified too closely here for fear of identifying the businessman and damaging his interests. The businessman presented this select gift at his audience with the Sultan, who was impressed and pleased. The businessman noticed as he left that the Sultan was hurrying over to the magnificent object to get a better look. But even a really special present does not always do the trick: the businessman ruefully admits he did not get the contract.

The salesmen who do get through and beat the competition tend to be those who are the real professionals at the game. That means people like Khashoggi. Khashoggi had a far more personal approach: he was willing to show the Sultan a good time, willing and eager to take the Sultan around London or bring a party to the Sultan's palace in Brunei. He gave every appearance of not needing the Sultan, but rather of being another rich man like the Sultan himself who just wanted to enjoy the Sultan's excellent company.

Not that Khashoggi did not use the gift tactic too. One of his presents was a special desk with electronic gadgets for the Sultan's study in the largest palace, the Istana Nurul Iman. It so happens that Khashoggi is closely connected with Mario Lavia who comes from Rome and has supplied hi-tech studies for the Sultan. Khashoggi had the advantage over ordinary businessmen, in that he was regularly in the business of supplying rich men's entertainment: he had the contacts, the organization and the back-up.

Khashoggi acted as agent or principal in buying the Sultan things which he wanted. Sometimes Khashoggi would suggest things which the Sultan might like to buy or lease. One little luxury supplied by Khashoggi was a Boeing 727. But not every sale which

Khashoggi made took the form of an object. He once persuaded the Sultan to guarantee a Swiss bank a loan of US$50 million to Khashoggi. Khashoggi gave the Sultan collateral in the form of an extraordinarily large and luxurious yacht. This yacht was so spectacular that it was used in the James Bond film *Never Say Never Again*.

The *Nabila*, named after Khashoggi's daughter, was completed in 1980. It is 282 feet long and included in its facilities a medical clinic, a hairdresser, a discothèque and a landing-pad for helicopters. The discothèque was capable of producing laser-beam spectacles and clouds of mist. Its ceiling had a mirrored-translucent deckhead (ceiling) with cinema projectors behind. The cinema-theatre was panelled in dark leather. The yacht incorporated three Otis lifts to save the passengers walking up and down stairs. And in addition to the main saloon and the dining saloon (where the deck-head was punctured by brass strips concealing lighting) there was an upper deck where sixty people could dine al fresco.

This monster of luxury was built by M. & B. Benetti and Canieri Navali Fratelli Benetti at Viareggio, Italy, to the designs of the builders themselves and Jon Bannenberg. It was powered by two 3,000 bhp 16-cylinder Nohab Polar turbo-charged diesel engines which gave it a cruising speed of about 17.5 knots. At this speed the vessel consumed 269 gallons an hour, including running the generator. A full tank contained 136,000 gallons of fuel.

Among the extensive electronic and other equipment were three Raytheon Mariner's Pathfinder radars and a Saturn-3 satellite-communication terminal with telephone facility, a Siemens telex machine and a Thomson-CFF Thomfax 3100 fax machine.

The accommodation included two master suites (his and hers), five large guest suites and four smaller ones. A crew of over fifty could sleep on board in the crew cabins. All the guest suites were named after precious stones (Lapis Lazuli, Topaz, Emerald, Ruby and so on) and varied in colour accordingly. The bathrooms were finished in onyx with large mirrored panels and gold-plated fittings. Many of the bathrooms had L-shaped baths on raised mezzanine areas. The bathrooms also had cylindrical-shaped showers and leather armchairs. The suites all had their own entertainment centres with colour televisions, video-cassette recorders and audio equipment. Many of the televisions were concealed in cabinets and raised electronically when required. Even the curtains were controlled electronically.

The *Nabila* was moored in Brunei for a long while. Khashoggi reportedly valued the yacht at U S$90 million (which would have given Khashoggi a good profit). He wanted to sell the *Nabila* to the Sultan but was refused, despite Khashoggi's persuasive talents. Perhaps the Sultan was getting wiser.

The Sultan certainly appeared willing to countenance alternative advice. The same Mario Lavia who supplied the hi-tech studies to the Sultan was also looking after the *Nabila* during some of its time in Brunei. The Sultan took a liking to Lavia and, according to one source, entrusted some hundreds of millions of dollars to his care. When Khashoggi next asked Lavia to do some work for him, Lavia was suddenly in a position to say 'no, thank you'.

Meanwhile Khashoggi had, nevertheless, persuaded the Sultan to guarantee the U S$50-million loan, using the yacht as security. Khashoggi went in default on the loan so, in 1985, the Sultan had to pay it off under the terms of the guarantee. This effectively gave him ownership of the yacht. The Sultan's representatives accordingly ousted Khashoggi and his partners from the Panamanian company, Silingroup Investments Inc., which owned the yacht. Then the yacht was offered for sale at the more realistic price of U S$35 million. Eventually it was sold to Donald Trump, the New York property developer, for U S$30 million. Clearly Khashoggi's valuation of U S$90 million had been a little ambitious. But then, Khashoggi did not make a fortune by understatement.

Before that denouement, Khashoggi had also tried to sell the Sultan another yacht – one that had yet to be built. This drawing-board yacht would have been even more spectacular and extraordinary than the *Nabila*. It was intended to be tremendously fast – with a top speed of some 70 miles per hour, powered by the same engines used to thrust forward a Boeing 747. The speed of this yacht was going to be so great that steel covers would be needed to protect the glass on the bridge. Since steering by sight would then be difficult, the captain would find his way with video cameras and radar.

The plans for this amazing yacht reached quite an advanced stage. They were scattered all over a room in the palace while the Sultan studied them. But in the end, nothing came of the idea and the plans were jettisoned. Instead the Sultan took delivery of his own luxury yacht, the *Khalifa*, which he bought quite independently of Khashoggi. Even Khashoggi could not win them all.

Another man who is a world-class salesman and has managed to get through to the Sultan is much less well known to the general public than Khashoggi. He is extremely discreet and private, to the extent that he has hardly ever appeared in any newspaper. Yet he is probably the doyen of all those who cater to the super-rich. Fabulously wealthy, with bases in London and Los Angeles, Bob Manoukian is a refugee from Armenia.

In London, he has a house in Knightsbridge, not very far from Harrods. It is 29 Pont Street, the former Danish Embassy on the corner of Pont Street and Cadogan Square. It has a swimming pool on the first floor and also contains both a 'gold room' and a 'silver room' filled with large numbers of objects made with each of these precious metals. If a wealthy visitor says he or she likes something in one of the rooms, the sculpture or whatever it is may well be sent round the next day. The bill is likely to follow later.

Bob Manoukian is credited by those who have seen him at work as the greatest salesman in the world. His technique is to find out what someone wants and then get it for him. Manoukian will go on talking and persuading until the target relents. If the target declines to tell Bob what he wants, that won't make any difference: Manoukian will find out. In the Sultan's case, Manoukian will also ask other people around the Sultan what currently interests the monarch. Even if the target and those around him do not know what he wants, that too can be overcome. Manoukian will tell him. He will say, 'Your Majesty, that corner there, it needs something. Now what does it need? Ah yes. It needs a larger-than-life-size model eagle with diamonds for eyes. Yes, that would be magnificent, don't you think?' If the target is incautious enough to agree, the eagle will be delivered. One such object which Manoukian managed to sell to the Sultan was a gold man riding a crystal horse set on a base of jade.

The young Sultan's passion for cars in the late seventies and early eighties played to one of Manoukian's particular strengths. He himself owns at least thirty cars, including eleven Rolls-Royces and Bentleys, seven Mercedes and four Ferraris. Manoukian used to change his Rolls-Royce Corniche every year. One year, though, when he went to Jack Barclay, the Rolls-Royce/Bentley dealer in Berkeley Square to change his car he found that his 'old' Rolls-Royce had only 400 miles on the clock; it looked better than the new one, too. So that year he kept his old Rolls-Royce.

Manoukian's lavish car collection is small compared to that of the Sultan. The royal fleet contains some 350 cars in all. The average value per car of the royal collection must be well over US$30,000 making their total value in excess of US$10 million. The collection was started by the Sultan's father, and so includes antique Rolls-Royces and Chevrolets. Each day the Sultan can choose which car to drive, as other people choose which tie to wear.

The Sultan prefers cars with two doors: four-door cars, he says, are for old men. The cars include such things as televisions, compact-disc players, drinks cabinets and much else besides. Manoukian has cars altered to suit the buyer. He tries to think of new gadgets that can be added so that his customers will have something unique. A recent new refinement is a car computer-telex machine.

To service all these cars there is a permanent team of engineers and maintenance men employed by the Sultan. In addition, engineers of the manufacturers fly out to visit. In early 1986, the men from Porsche in Stuttgart, West Germany, were making a service call to Brunei.

The Sultan's favourite car of late has been a crimson two-door Mercedes with white leather seats and steering wheel. In place of a number plate there is a royal crest in gold. One of his Aston Martins has a gold plaque on it, saying, 'Built specially for His Royal Highness, the Sultan of Brunei'.

Bob Manoukian has also made sales to the Sultan to help him enjoy an even more expensive hobby than luxury cars – aeroplanes. In 1986, Manoukian was working on a special order from the Sultan. The Sultan had decided that what he really needed was a custom-fitted Boeing 727. Manoukian was only too pleased to oblige. A great deal of gold and mink was put into the plane; fibre optics were used for various gadgets and, at a press of a button, various essentials like a telex machine would emerge from their places. The plane was even fitted with a jacuzzi, despite the problems that they can cause in aeroplanes. Requiring a large volume of water, which weighs a great deal, the siting of the water tank and the jacuzzi itself affect the balance of the aeroplane. Incidentally, it is a legal requirement that the jacuzzi must be capable of being emptied in seven and a half seconds. Gravity is not enough, so the water has to be pumped out. The sucking of the pump is so powerful that it is dangerous to get close to the plughole. Unfortunately, when this luxurious plane, complete with fast emptying jacuzzi, was finally delivered, the Sultan was not wholly satisfied. So he disposed of it. Manoukian has also sold paintings to the Sultan. The Sultan and his family have acquired (though not all through Manoukian) quite a collection of Impressionist paintings, including several Monets, a Van Gogh and various works by Pissarro, Sisley and Renoir. The Sultan has also aquired some earlier paintings, including one by the nineteenth-century French neo-classicist Jean-Léon Gérome.

As if sales of *objets d'art*, paintings, cars and planes were not enough, Manoukian also sells clothes to the Sultan. Manoukian has retail shops in London, selling clothes under the brand name of 'Vincci'. There are three Vincci shops, all within fifty yards of each other in Jermyn Street in the traditional clubland district of St James's. But there is nothing traditionally British about the Vincci shops: the name Vincci sounds Italian, and many of the goods are indeed Italian. One other special characteristic of the shops is that the assistant and his colleagues selling formal menswear are particularly large. Somehow they look far more well-muscled than most clothes salesmen. Nevertheless, they will readily let you have a belt for £295 or a suit for £695. Shoes start at £250 a pair and go a long way up. Frankly, they would rather you did not bother to go in unless you are extremely wealthy. But if you are in the multimillionaire class, they are willing to bring a selection of fifty suits round to you at your London residence or hotel suite. That would be the normal way for Vincci or anyone else to sell clothes to the Sultan, who would not be expected actually to visit the shop, like a common mortal.

One might think that Vincci's high prices would be reflected in a very large profit margin. But no. According to the 1984 accounts, the gross mark-up is a moderate 66 per cent, and the net profit a mere 1 per cent of turnover. As with the Belfry, on the basis of the accounts, one wonders why the owner bothers with the business at all. And as with the Belfry, the holding-company is offshore. The Belfry holding-company was in Panama, that of Vincci is in Liechtenstein.

Incidentally, the accountants who audited the figures for 1984 saw fit to write in their report:

> In common with many businesses of similar size and organization the company's system of control is dependent upon the close involvement of the director. Where independent confirmation of the completeness of the accounting records was therefore not available we have accepted assurances from the director that all the company's transactions have been reflected in the records.

Manoukian often stays at the best suite in the Sheraton-Utama Hotel in Brunei, which is the only top-class hotel there. He visits for a month at a time to promote his services to the Sultan, but the Sultan's business is so valuable to Manoukian that one of his three brothers stays semi-permanently in Brunei, keeping open the channel of communication, ready to pass on to Bob the latest whim that the Sultan may express.

Selling to the Sultan is clearly not a job for the half-hearted. Sending a brochure in the post and hoping for an order is a waste of time. The successful salesmen are international professionals at the job. Whether or not these luxury yachts, modified cars and all the other knick-knacks are really worth all this dedication by grown men is another matter. But people keep on trying to find ways to make a sale. They will try anything, even riding a horse, carrying a stick and hitting a wooden ball . . .

CHAPTER SIX

Anyone for Polo?

_____ ے _____

> As long as there are rich people in the world, they will be desirous of distinguishing themselves from the poor.
> Rousseau, *A Discourse on Political Economy*, 1758

One of the ways for salesmen and others to ingratiate themselves with the Sultan has been to send to Brunei someone who plays polo. The idea is that the polo-playing emissary will get a game or two with the Sultan and thus come to know him socially. From that informal introduction, business may follow.

After the event, it is usually denied by the businessmen and nations and others who send polo players that their emissary was deliberately chosen for his skill at the game. They protest it was pure coincidence. If so, Brunei is the location for the most extraordinary coincidental concentration of polo players the world has ever known. Jardine Fleming, a leading Hong Kong financial institution, sent a polo-playing man to Brunei. He stayed for six months, but he didn't get a contract. He didn't even get a game. Polo in Brunei is by royal invitation only.

One man who 'happened' to be a polo player was the previous British High Commissioner, Francis Cornish. In this instance, it might really be a coincidence (or else a miscalculation by the Foreign and Commonwealth Office). Cornish, a former aide-de-camp of Prince Charles, arrived in Brunei and at his first audience with the Sultan he was asked when he would like to play. To the surprise of the Sultan and everyone else, he replied that he did not intend to play at all. Either the fact that Cornish is a practised polo player had nothing to do with his appointment or else the Foreign Office wrongly assumed he would make use of this important attribute. Possibly Cornish thought that if he started playing polo in Brunei he would end up wasting a lot of time playing the game. But one could argue that there could be no better use of his time than forging close relations with the royal family. Cornish clearly did not think so.

Two British jewellery shops use the polo strategy. Garrard is the grandest of traditional jewellers in Britain because it proudly carries the tag, 'the Crown Jewellers'. Asprey also has royal connections, holding the commission to supply various kinds of objects to various members of the British royal family. Asprey supplies all sorts of luxury goods, including jewellery, silver, leather-bound books, gold toothbrushes and custom-made ornaments, including a silver-gilt sculpture of a toasted triple-decker egg sandwich. Both Garrard and Asprey have made many sales to the Sultan and to cement the relationship both shops take a polo team over to Brunei to play against the Sultan for a prize given by the shops. Naturally, the teams shipped out by the shops normally lose, but they clearly think the Sultan's business is worth all the effort and expense.

In his initial enthusiasm for polo, the Sultan played a great deal. He had started to take an interest in the game in the mid-seventies, and received his first shipment of ponies in Brunei in 1976; games started being held there in 1977. In 1980 he took a Brunei team abroad for the first time, to Singapore.

In Brunei, he created a new polo ground in the Jerudong district with a large club-house and a lovely swimming pool surrounded by changing rooms. There is stabling for the polo ponies, much of which is air-conditioned. There is also a grandstand with a private section (also air-conditioned) for the royal family. A hilly little golf course is on one side, next to the sea, and there are three polo fields. The cost of this beautiful country club was some Singapore $30 million (equivalent in early 1986 to about £9.4 million).

The economics of polo are such that it is only for the very rich. A single top-class pony can cost US$15,000. In theory one needs six ponies, one for each chukka, or period of play. Most people get by on less though, riding, say, three ponies in two chukkas each. A typical amateur will probably only own two ponies himself and will borrow the third. Even so, the outlay can still be US$30,000 for two ponies with limited playing lives. The ponies need to be trained, exercised, fed and sheltered, all at great expense. The rider also needs equipment and must pay for a club membership. Then there is the cost of transporting the ponies to away-games and paying for the vet when the ponies are ill or injured. This is why polo is a game for the rich. And this is why polo has a special prestige: it separates the rich from ordinary people.

The expense is so great that even the Prince of Wales, Prince Charles, finds it convenient for his polo-playing expenses to be subsidized by a sponsor. His sponsor used to be Guy Wildenstein, the French art dealer, but now it is Geoffrey Kent, who is married to a multi-millionairess. The cost of Kent's subsidy of the Prince of Wales's polo team in 1987 was reportedly US$384,000. The Sultan of Brunei, however, pays all his own expenses, and many of the expenses of visiting teams as well.

The Sultan has acquired over 200 ponies; perhaps as many as 300. The cost of buying the ponies was high, since the Sultan bought them all in a hurry, and he may have had to pay a premium. But even if they cost only US$15,000 each, his total bill would still have been US$3 million, and on top of that came the transport costs for the many ponies that were flown in.

The transportation of polo ponies, incidentally, is not a worry-free exercise. If the valuable ponies become agitated, they can be very dangerous in an aircraft, unbalancing it or smashing a hole through the side of the pressurized cabin. Guns are issued to those looking after them, and if a pony gets out of control it must be shot dead. An ordinary gun would propel its bullet through the horse and the side of the aircraft, so the gun is specially designed: the bullet is tied to the gun to prevent it going too far, and it then explodes inside the horse, to make death certain.

If polo generally differentiates the rich from the ordinary, the way the Sultan practises and plays differentiates him from the rich. When he practises hitting the ball while riding, he does not, as others do, hit the ball, ride after it and swing at it again. Instead, he has a man with a bag of balls running alongside who throws a ball down whenever he needs one.

Then again, if the pitch is wet it is not every polo player who can call on a few helicopters to hover over the pitch to evaporate the water — as the Sultan has done. Nor does everyone have a team of servants to come onto the pitch with sponges and buckets to sponge the earth dry. The Sultan has commanded this too.

In the early 1980s, the Sultan instituted an annual international polo tournament. Teams from a number of countries around the world, including the United States, Hong Kong and the Philippines were invited on terms which they found hard to refuse. Their accommodation in Brunei was free, transport in some cases was free, the ponies were provided and there was every prospect of fine polo in luxurious surroundings. The main drawback was the unwillingness of the Sultan or his assistants to let him lose a single game.

The Sultan used 'hired assassins', a gruesome title given to professional polo players, normally Argentinians, who are so good that if you put a few on your team you have an excellent chance of winning even if you yourself just sit on your pony and walk round in circles.

Hired assassins have the top handicap of 10 (that is 10 goals given to the opposing side). By comparison, the Sultan of Brunei has a handicap of 3, which is good for a non-professional. (The Prince of Wales has a handicap of 4.) The professionals who reach a handicap of 10 consider themselves and are considered as stars. They each get in the region of U S$5,000 for a day's work plus U S$1,000 for each goal scored by the team they play for. Their attitude to their employers tends to be, 'When we play the game, just keep out of the way and we will score the goals.'

The Sultan of Brunei won some games against one of the Malaysian Sultans with the aid of such sporting prima donnas. But then the Malaysians too started hiring the 'assassins' and were able to hold their own again. One may wonder what was the point of it all.

One polo player tells of a game in which he played against a Brunei team that included the Sultan. The visiting players found that, after two of the six chukkas, they were doing well. They had a higher handicap but had scored more goals, bringing the score level at 5 goals all. That meant that if the game continued in the same vein, one would have expected the visitors to go on scoring more goals and win. But when the ponies were changed as normal at the end of the second chukka, the visitors suddenly found themselves on inferior animals. They proceeded to lose by the overwhelming margin of 19 to 6, only managing to score one more goal in the last four chukkas.

In April 1986, a team visited Brunei from Australia. It may be pure coincidence, but the team lost heavily (16–0) in a mid-week game in which the Sultan was playing on the other side. But on the Saturday, when the Sultan was not playing, the visitors and hosts battled in an extremely close game.

Some people now stay away because of the way the odds are stacked against them. Others continue going because they are looked after very generously in other respects. As one said, 'It's a freebie, so most accept it.' Much depends on how highly the individuals value their pride – something which may receive another test. The attitude expected of most visitors is subservience. This kind of behaviour comes naturally to the professional flatterers and the overawed, but many on the international polo circuit are neither one nor the other. They are independently wealthy people who consider it beneath them to be subservient to anyone. A lot of them come from second, third or later generations of wealth in their family, so they are often used to mixing with rich people. And since polo itself is so popular among royalty, they may be used to royalty too. Some of these do not like to be 'accommodating hand and foot', as one of them called it.

The strange character of polo in Brunei reached some kind of extreme in 1984, soon after Brunei celebrated its full independence from Britain. The Agong (King) of Malaysia, who was the former Sultan of Pahang, brought a team to play against the Sultan's team, which consisted of himself, his brother Prince Jefri, an extremely good player for an amateur, and two 'hired assassins'. The Malaysian team consisted of two sons of the Agong together with another two 'assassins'. The two umpires were also top professionals. This had the potential to be an extremely competitive, high class game.

Before the game had progressed far, there was a diversion. Adnan

Khashoggi's wife and his beautiful daughter Nabila arrived some twenty minutes after the start. The small stand was already reasonably full, mainly with the local Muslim elite and their wives. Mrs Khashoggi and Nabila arrived at the bottom of the stand and walked up the aisle between the spectators, both late arrivals wearing see-through blouses. According to someone present, the crowd was stunned. The women spectators looked at the fronts of the Khashoggi women and then looked quickly at their husbands. The husbands looked at the fronts of the Khashoggi women and then looked at the sky or their feet or even at the game. Inside the darkened windows that surrounded the royal box, members of the royal family could be seen leaning across to see what was going on.

The game, meanwhile, was indeed turning out to be close and exciting. By the sixth chukka, the score was seven all and the game was coming to a tense climax, with much personal and national pride at stake. Then, some thirty yards from the Pahang family's goal, the Brunei side committed a foul. That, at least, is how it appeared from the stand. In fact it appeared that the Sultan himself had committed the foul. But to the surprise of some spectators, one of the two umpires maintained that it was the Pahang side which had committed the foul. One of the umpires, incidentally, worked full-time for the Sultan in Brunei while the other sold him ponies.

Since the two umpires disagreed, they rode over to the referee at the side of the pitch for him to arbitrate. The referee, Enrique Zobel, a man of substance who had played polo with the Sultan himself, told them that the Brunei side had fouled. The umpires rode back to the players. But something must have happened as they rode back. Perhaps they suddenly remembered where their best interests lay. When they reached the players, instead of awarding the penalty to Pahang, they awarded it to Brunei.

Enrique Zobel rang the bell to stop the game. The umpires came back across to him and he told them in no uncertain terms that Brunei had fouled and the penalty should be awarded to Pahang. The umpires rode back to the players and still awarded the penalty to Brunei. Zobel was so disgusted that he stormed off. The Pahang visitors were furious. The spectators who knew their polo were shocked that the two well-known professionals acting as umpires should behave so badly. And the Brunei team, which accordingly received a penalty to be taken only thirty yards from the Pahang goal, was able to score a goal and thus win the match.

The significant footnote to this bizarre sporting encounter is that Zobel, the referee, was the man who made the most spectacular sale to the Sultan after getting to know him better on the polo field: a contract to build the biggest palace ever created.

CHAPTER SEVEN

The Biggest Palace in the World

───────── ☌ ─────────

Superfluous wealth can buy superfluities only.
                    Henry David Thoreau, *Walden*, 1854

Enrique 'EZ' (pronounced 'easy') Zobel is a 'Mestizo', that is to say, a Filipino of Spanish descent. The Mestizos tend to consider themselves superior to other Filipinos and have greater education and wealth. Zobel maintains the Spanish connection, being involved in a major luxury-property development in Sotogrande, Southern Spain, twenty minutes' drive from Gibraltar.

At the beginning of the 1980s, 'EZ' was chief executive of Ayala Corporation, the bluest of blue-chip companies in the Philippines, owning most of the land in the business district of Metro-Manila. Ayala was and is still acknowledged to have some of the best management talent in the Philippines.

Zobel is a fiercely independent and proud man – as his ruling against the Sultan in the polo match demonstrates. None the less, during the years in which Ferdinand Marcos was in power in the Philippines, Zobel was on familiar terms with the President. It was because of this fact that a notorious Central Intelligence Agency operation in Hawaii thought it worth cultivating him. When Zobel went to play polo in Hawaii, he would fall into conversation with Ronald Rewald. Rewald was a CIA agent who had learned to play polo precisely and exclusively so that he could chat in a casual way to well-placed people such as Zobel. Rewald would be taking mental notes while Zobel talked about what Marcos had said to him recently.

Ironically, while the CIA was using the polo strategy on Zobel, Zobel was simultaneously using the polo strategy on Sultan Hassanal Bolkiah. Zobel went over to Brunei for polo numerous times, sometimes taking companions with him. The Sultan also made trips to the Philippines, which is only a relatively short jet-ride away. The Sultan would sometimes transport his polo ponies there and back.

Good relations between Zobel and the Brunei royal family were already well established. Zobel was one of only two foreigners allowed to establish a bank in Brunei. Zobel's creation was the 'Island Development Bank'. The Sultan's brother, Prince Mohamed, was a director. Then in 1985 the Prince's stake was sold to Princess Rashidah, the Sultan's eldest daughter.

Zobel is not so proud that he is above using some flattery to get business with the Sultan. He commissioned a massive book, called *The Sultan of Brunei*, which celebrated the Sultan's life and background. The book is massive not because it has much detail but because it has enormous colour pictures and large type. It is surprisingly frank in parts and yields the revelation that Hassanal 'had to be practically abducted' to become Sultan. Otherwise it views the Sultan's virtues through a magnifying glass but finds his vices obscured behind a stone wall. The Sultan is said to have shown himself to be 'clever' at the Victorian Institution, although the records clearly show he was two years behind for his age. Brunei itself is also flattered with the compliment of showing 'fierce bravery, a bravery of which Spaniards had proof in the Sixteenth Century, when they failed to gain a colonial foothold in Brunei'. The fact that the Bruneians fled into the jungle before the Spanish forces is omitted, as is the fact that disease, not Bruneian bravery, made the Spanish depart.

Thus through polo, flattery and his status in the Philippines, Zobel was able to obtain business from the Sultan. Zobel's contract to build the Istana Nurul Iman was his biggest coup. The Sultan did consider putting the contract out to tender, which would have been the normal practice for such a major design and building project. But Zobel persuaded the Sultan that the business of tendering would take up too much valuable time. The quickest solution would be to let 'EZ' handle it all. In view of the size of the project one would assume that a great deal of time and thought would go into it. But no, the biggest palace on earth was built in a headlong rush.

The Sultan wanted to have the palace ready for the celebration of full independence from Britain in early 1984. The design and construction was a race against time. There was simply not long enough to reflect carefully on the concept and design of the palace.

Zobel quickly hired the most prominent architect in the Philippines, Leandro V. Locsin. Locsin was and remains a first-class exponent of uncompromisingly modern architecture. He was for a long time the preferred architect of Imelda Marcos, the wife of the former Philippines' President, who commissioned him to design a number of striking structures in Manila, including the prominent former Cultural Centre in Manila and the Philippine Plaza Hotel. Locsin is the main reason Manila has a higher proportion of stylish modern buildings than any other capital of South-East or East Asia.

Unfortunately, Locsin's aggressive modern design would turn out not to be totally consistent with the Sultan's taste. This would cause enough difficulties, but what made it worse was that Locsin did not have sufficient contact with his ultimate client, the Sultan. Zobel enforced his position as the main contractor and kept to himself most of the contact with the Sultan.

Nevertheless, excited by the new commission, the design team at Locsin's company worked fast to produce two alternative concepts for the palace. They had two weeks. They ran this sprint under something of a handicap. Not only had they never had the chance to talk to the Sultan about what he wanted, they had never even seen the site. Still, the team came up with two designs. One of them was ultra-modern – a palace that would be a grand set-piece of twentieth-century modernism, just as St Peter's in Rome had been a grand set-piece of sixteenth- and seventeenth-century Renaissance and Baroque design. The ultra-modern design was probably the one Locsin favoured himself to make his name in architectural history. The alternative was a compromise. It was still modern but it had more detail and some typically Islamic motifs that softened the modernity. When the two designs were put before the Sultan, it was the less radical design that he chose. It was a clue to the

Sultan's taste but not a clue that fitted in with Locsin's long-established style.

In the next stage of design, Locsin, as was natural for him, removed some of the details, making even this alternative design very modern.

Perhaps because the designers did not see the site before designing the building, the palace was not well suited to the location. The main feature of the design was the long sloping roofs like the roofs of the long houses which were common in the jungle of Brunei. This design looks good from above. Unfortunately, the site is on the top of a hill, so everybody has to look up at it from below. As a result, the long sloping roofs were bound to seem almost like a continuation of the hill. The only place from which to see the roofs from a good angle would be an aircraft.

The construction of the biggest palace in the world was chaotic. It is really not surprising given that the contractor had only two years to take the palace from the drawing-board to completion. The specification included 1,778 rooms, most of which had to be supplied with lighting, air-conditioning, wall-coverings and other decorations and fittings. There were times when work was being done on the floor and ceiling of a room at the same time. There were leaks. The electric cables in at least some parts of the palace were not placed in ducts, as would normally be the case, but were just set in the plaster wall-coverings.

Bechtel, the American company, was called in to add its expertise on large-scale projects, and employees of Bechtel went to Manila to advise. They came with their wives and stayed at the better hotels, running up per diem costs, which Zobel did not appreciate. Zobel was working to a budget believed to be U S$350 million and was very concerned about it. Presumably he had told the Sultan a fixed price and was keen to build the palace for that price and still make a good profit. Thus, absurd as it may seem, the most luxurious residence in the world was built with an eye on the pennies.

One expensive item was the roof of the throne hall. Originally it was going to be made in pre-stressed concrete, but in view of the vast expanse to be covered, Bechtel recommended it should be made of steel. They made a computer analysis to design it. This kind of roof, on this scale, had never been attempted before.

46

Legions of Filipino workers were shipped in. They were put in temporary accommodation on the work-site, without air-conditioning. The Filipinos discovered that workers from other parts of the world were being paid a great deal more than they were, and they went on strike. It was said that the strike was (or could be made) illegal. But the Filipinos were not concerned with the law. If the Sultan wanted the palace finished the workers would have to be paid more. He did. So they were.

Extra costs such as this and the Bechtel expenses began to squeeze Zobel's budget. Suddenly some parts of the specification fell by the wayside. Originally, all the interior walls were to be covered in marble. That was dropped. There was originally going to be a private hospital or clinic. That building remained empty. There was going to be a water-tank inside the golden dome which presides over the whole complex. That got flushed away too.

Bechtel received an initial estimate of US$17 million for the thirty-eight different kinds of marble. One particular marble, travertine, was to clad the entire outside of the palace. With Zobel trying to save every cent possible, his own people relieved Bechtel of the task of buying this marble and went to Italy themselves. They changed the specification somewhat and ended up paying 'only' US$10 million.

Eventually, Zobel made a further saving by switching Bechtel from being joint-contractor to being supplier of executives on secondment. But his other costs were still rising. To meet the deadline, his men had to work overtime and that meant higher rates of pay.

These tales of rising costs and squeezed budgets raise the question of whether Zobel was out of pocket at the end of the day. But the view of one person involved on the project is that profits made by both Zobel and Bechtel were very satisfactory indeed.

Despite the frenzied rush to design and build it, the strike and the cutbacks, the biggest palace in the world is still an amazing building. Its size alone is astonishing. It is bigger than Buckingham Palace, the Vatican or any other palace. The Istana Nurul Iman is certainly original. The vast roofs are elegant and subtly curving (even though this is not easily appreciated from ground level). The public areas make a spectacular use of space. The approach to the house is a long drive that ingloriously circles round the back of the palace and then sweeps up a hill to the main entrance. An honoured visitor gets out of his car next to a few extremely wide steps and walks up to an equally wide entrance area with marble archways and sixteen-foot high carved wooden doors permanently guarded by at least two soldiers.

Through the wooden doors is a wide promenade. On the left is a little island in which a small orchestra plays music. (To get across the water the orchestra goes underground and then climbs up some stairs into the island.) Continuing straight ahead, the visitor passes between pools, fountains, cascades and interior gardens. Then he comes to the stairs and escalators (reminiscent of a hotel) leading up to three public rooms: a reception room in the middle, the throne hall on the left and the royal banquet hall on the right.

The throne hall is vast. It has four thrones (the extra two are in case of visits by royal couples). Twelve astonishingly large chandeliers, each weighing one ton, hang from the very high ceiling. Behind the four thrones is a sixty-foot high Islamic-style arch with two more arches within the main arch. All of them are covered with 22-carat gold tiles. It is a breathtaking sight.

The royal banquet hall seats 4,000 and, like the other three rooms, has the concave curving ceiling of the traditional Borneo longhouse. Again there are large chandeliers and Islamic arches covered in gold. The reception hall is also tremendously high, with yet more gold-covered arches and a light-coloured shining marble floor with a strong geometric pattern in black.

Nearby is the Privy Council Chamber, with Moroccan onyx marble along one of its walls which, so it is claimed, was carved from the last block of such marble in the world. Royal 'suites' (which are each the equivalent in accommodation to a large house) are provided for members of the royal family present and future. The suites consist in all of 900 rooms.

The sporting complex has a swimming pool, tennis, squash and badminton courts and a polo practice ground.

In addition to the state rooms and the private rooms, there are also government offices and many reception rooms. In all, the total number of rooms is either 1,778 or 1,788 (different figures have been given at different times). The total floor space is 2.2 million square feet, the equivalent to just over 50 acres (20.5 hectares). The floor space is equivalent to that of 2,450 ordinary semi-detached houses.

Given the royal family's love of cars, a lot of parking space has been provided. The figure is variously given as 695 or 843 spaces. Less important visitors come into the palace via the underground car park which, like all underground car parks, is a rather depressing place.

Roads 3.1 miles long have been constructed for access to the palace. There are 257 toilets and the sewage-treatment plant can handle 300,000 gallons per day (which is what 1,500 people might be expected to flush away). There are 18 lifts and 44 staircases.

The chandeliers, big and small, number 564. They and the other light fittings take an astonishing total of 51,490 light bulbs. That means that if the light bulbs were to last, say, one year, a servant could change 200 bulbs a day and at the end of the year would have to start changing them all over again.

Thirty-one countries have provided supplies for the construction of the palace. The countries range from Sweden to Ethiopia and from the United States to Yugoslavia. Brazil and the Philippines supplied much of the wood, and Italy naturally provided most of the marble which covers 600,597 square feet – equivalent to 14 acres (5.6 hectares).

The thirty-eight kinds of marble include seven kinds of travertine, two kinds of onyx, three botticinos, three rossos, two Isolas and three calacatas. The list runs from azul bahia through marron visener and ends with travertine scuro.

The varieties of marble, the imagination-defying size of the palace and the luxury of some of its fittings, did not, of course, make everybody like it.

Expatriate residents of Brunei have observed that one side of the palace, where the residential suites overlook the river and Kampong Ayer, looks distinctly like a multi-storey car park. Among international publications which reviewed it, the French newspaper *Le Monde* was haughty, referring to '*son faste – parfois d'un goût cont-*

estable' (which can be loosely translated as 'its pomp – sometimes of doubtful taste'). The American magazine *House and Garden* conceded, 'The interiors certainly do not lack for the kind of astounding glamor and exoticism that one has come to the ends of the earth in search of.' But the article went on, 'It is impossible . . . not to be reminded of *The Wizard of Oz* as one approaches the golden mosaic triple arch that surrounds the doorway to the throne hall, or not to think of *The King and I* as one slowly advances toward the gilded, wing-eaved canopy beneath which the Sultan and his Queen sit on state occasions.'

The fact is that, despite its virtues, the palace tends towards the gaudy, and the independent media of the world was not inhibited in pointing this out.

The media coverage of the palace naturally missed a great deal of what had happened, partly because the main theme of the stories was, inevitably, astonishment at such a huge and expensive construction. Newspapers at that time did not know that the design and construction had taken place in such difficult circumstances. One of the points missed was how the building was not actually finished. Zobel's men failed to meet the deadline and even as late as 1986 there were still rooms that had not been plastered. More strikingly, within two years of the supposed completion the plaster was coming away in some rooms and repairs were necessary. In the great rush, mistakes had been made. The largest palace in the world was, in part, a botched job. The Sultan himself was unhappy with some of the fittings that had been used and the way they had been installed in the last-minute rush and cost-cutting.

That the whole palace had been misconceived in the first place soon became more clear. The specially selected and ordered furniture and fittings began to be changed. Dale Keller, a designer of international repute, had been brought in to do the interior design. He was a friend of Locsin and they shared a liking for very simple modern design. The two had worked on other commissions together. Keller's interior designs were dramatic and modern in the same way as Locsin's structural design, but clearly this modernity was not to the taste of the ultimate users.

The taste of the Sultan, or perhaps that of his first wife, Queen

Saleha, appeared to be poles apart from that of Locsin and Keller. Gradually the custom-made furniture was consigned to the basement storeroom and replaced by chairs and tables in Louis XVI and other antique styles. The sleek structural design remained in place of course, as did much of the furnishings, such as the wall-claddings and carpets. But instead of these blending with modern furniture, they were clashing with antiques and reproduction antiques.

Perhaps the Sultan himself recognized how unfortunate was this mixture of styles, because he has since then completely gutted some rooms and replaced them with decor of a traditional English sort. Subsequently he has gone on to refurnish his study with modern gadgets supplied by Lavia and the hi-tech desk given by Khashoggi.

Ever since it was built, the palace has been in a constant state of redesign and rebuilding. In 1986, the Sultan was having a complete new suite of rooms built for himself at a level above the existing suites.

Following the building of the Istana Nurul Iman, Enrique Zobel appeared to fall out of favour with the Sultan. But not for long. He resurfaced and obtained the contract for some of the new works at the palace. Back in the Philippines, his fortunes slumped. After an argument with powerful members of his own family, he left his job as chief of the Ayala Corporation and had to make do with buying out its international operations. To make matters even worse, he declared himself in favour of President Marcos only weeks before the election that led to the defeat of Marcos and to his exile in Hawaii. Naturally Zobel is unpopular with the new regime headed by President Corazon Aquino.

International reaction to the Istana Nurul Iman was mixed. But the Sultan, it seems, was offended. He took his palace seriously and did not like even mild criticism. He wanted the publicity to stop. Locsin, the architect, naturally remained keen for coverage of his largest work. He wanted to have his creation reported in the specialist magazines of design and architecture. He assisted the American magazine *Connoisseur* with a feature on the building. The article was one of the most complimentary, ending, '. . . the New Istana must be judged a grand success'.

But the Sultan issued a writ, claiming that Locsin was in breach of the terms of his contract. Under the contract, no details of the building were supposed to be released. It appears, though, that what really annoyed the Sultan was not the colour pictures of the palace or the generally uncritical prose alongside. What irritated him was mention of the price. *Connoisseur* said the budget was US$250 million and that it had been 'vastly exceeded'. The Sultan's concern seems to have been that the people of Brunei, many of whom are very poor by Western standards, would be provoked by such expense. It is also possible that he was concerned that his father, too, might consider such an outlay misguided.

Misguided? Yes, it might have been. But the Sultan is in the position that he can make a mistake costing vastly in excess of US$250 million and it does not really matter. Since the creation of this enormous palace did not go too well, what was he to do? Build another, of course!

CHAPTER EIGHT

A Family Inbred

We may see the small value God has for riches by the people he gives them to.

> Alexander Pope, 'Thoughts on various subjects', 1727

A major influence on the Sultan has always been and still remains his extensive family.

The Sultan's family is easy to regard as a kind of soap opera. The wealth is there, so is the strong family life. And when the ratings begin to fall, someone in the family can be relied upon to do something sufficiently extravagant or bizarre to bring back the viewers. The family also has a continuing source of tension and contrast, which can be relied upon to produce conflict and offence on a regular basis. This division, to simplify, is between the devout traditionalists and the playboys. The large family also has an embarrassing weakness that occasionally comes back to haunt them. The family is inbred. This is probably the cause of some of their oddities and problems.

The inbreeding appears to have been encouraged by the Sultan's father, the Seri Begawan, since at least three of his children married their cousins. The Sultan himself married Raja Saleha, his brother Mohamed married Pengiran Anak Zariah and his sister Umi Kalthun married Pengiran Anak Idris. The cousins they married are all brothers and sisters of each other. The problems created by this tradition of inbreeding have become so great that the family has been advised to stop.

In the division between the more austere in the family and the more self-indulgent, the Sultan himself ranks as the most powerful of the self-indulgent sort. His father disapproved of some of the Sultan's activities and, as will become clear later, this would ultimately lead to a serious family rift – a crystallization of the basic conflict. The devout traditionalists of the family are those who follow in the footsteps of the Sultan's father, the Seri Begawan. The leader of these is the oldest of the Sultan's brothers and the closest to being a rival, Prince Mohamed.

Prince Mohamed has unfortunate looks. He has a large thick face and a wispy moustache. His lower teeth settle ahead of his upper teeth. He is only a couple of years younger than the Sultan and, according to his performance at school, is more intelligent. He has been obliged to live with being number two to his brother all his life, and the two brothers have not always been very close.

Some people regard Mohamed as the brother who would have made the best Sultan. They regard the fact that his older brother is on the throne as an unfortunate accident of birth. For them Prince Mohamed is much more serious, hard-working and sensible. Among Prince Mohamed's great virtues, say those who approve of him, is that he is polite: he inquires after other people's well-being and he remembers who they are. He is a devout Muslim and was respectful to his father. He frequently visits other countries in his role of Foreign Minister, making bilateral visits and attending international conferences. Prince Mohamed also spends a lot of time with his wife, Pengiran Anak Zariah, and thus presents a more stable image. His wife, meanwhile, is close to the Sultan's wife, Queen Saleha, who is, of course, her sister. These three, Mohamed, Zariah and Queen Saleha, represent a grouping unified by a generally traditional outlook.

This favourable view of Mohamed is not universally shared. Some regard Prince Mohamed as grim and slightly odd. While he may be intelligent by the standards of his family, few would call him an intellectual. When playing polo, he does not show anything like the gusto and relish of his brother Prince Jefri. Overweight and sluggish, he sometimes seems hardly to have the energy to keep up with the play and trails behind looking none too happy.

His dress sense is overblown. He seems to have a strong penchant for wearing white. He wears such things as a double-breasted white suit and a loud tie to a formal dinner. One particular white outfit gave rise to the comment, by insiders in the court who are certainly not his admirers, that he looked like a professional magician.

His diet is a little unusual too. When attending the meeting of the Association of South-East Asian Nations in Singapore in June 1987, Prince Mohamed stayed at the Marina Mandarin Hotel and ate seafood for every meal – breakfast, lunch and supper.

Prince Mohamed is undoubtedly a devout Muslim. But there is eccentricity in his spiritual beliefs too. When he takes delivery of a new car, he has it specially washed and blessed. On one occasion he had an accident when he hit the rear of a car that had stopped on the other side of a humpbacked bridge. He was furious with the man who had washed and blessed his car: the man, he decided, had not prayed well enough. After the car was repaired and repainted, Prince Mohamed had it washed and blessed a second time. He insisted that on this occasion the job be done properly. (The man must have done a better job as, since then, the Prince has not had any further accidents in that car.)

In the family spectrum, Prince Mohamed is the sober, austere one. But everything is relative.

When it comes to cars, all the brothers are enthusiasts. Mohamed apparently likes cars in white too. One is a custom-built white Mercedes. Among the many extras are wing mirrors that are not in fact wing mirrors at all. Instead of having silvered glass in them they have miniature video cameras. The pictures taken by these cameras are projected on to a screen on the dashboard in front of the Prince. If he wants to direct the cameras to the left or right, or zoom in on something behind him, he simply presses the appropriate controls. Meanwhile, the bodywork of the car is completely different from that of the normal Mercedes and the sides are much wider, to accommodate tyres the width of those on racing cars.

At the other end of the spectrum in the family is Prince Jefri. Jefri is even more of a hedonist than the Sultan, and he is closest to him. They often travel together. The Sultan has made Prince Jefri the head of the most sensitive ministry for a wealthy country, the Ministry of Finance. Jefri is the youngest brother who presents no threat to the Sultan, and is hence liked and trusted. The Sultan is dominant and both of them are happy with that. Mohamed would not be content with the same sort of relationship.

Again in contrast to Mohamed, Prince Jefri is handsome, and his moustache makes him look dashing. He plays polo with such élan that professionals in the business think that with sufficient practice he could become one of them. Each morning he darts through the capital of Brunei in his black Porsche, two motorcycle outriders go ahead of him with sirens blaring to clear the way, while an official black car brings up the rear.

Prince Jefri has the air of an untamed animal, ruthless but effortlessly attractive, like the archetypal hero of a romantic novel. He appears the sort of man whom the heroines of such novels pursue because they think that they alone may be able to tame him.

Prince Jefri and the younger members of the Pahang royal family sometimes get together and form a veritable elite team of pleasure-seekers. The Prince has been a particularly keen party-goer at his beach villa, with girls from various parts of the world. He is not unaware of his attractions, and he dresses as though he has walked out of a couturier's via a gold merchant. While Mohamed's dress sense is faintly reminiscent of Marshal Goering, Jefri's is closer to that of Richard Gere.

One expatriate living in the capital says that when the motorcycle sirens blare, the secretaries in his office rush to the windows to catch a glimpse of the Prince's sultry good looks. If the siren turns out to be blaring for Prince Mohamed, they turn back from the window in disappointment. On one occasion when Prince Jefri appeared in a procession, girls along the route shouted out his name as though he were a pop star.

Despite Prince Jefri's attractions for the opposite sex, he is, like the Sultan himself, extremely shy. In fact, he hardly ever speaks in public and generally keeps to a few friends. One of these friends, incidentally, is Bob Manoukian.

Prince Jefri's sense of fun has got him into one or two scrapes. His wife, Princess Noorhayati, spends much of her time in London and so do their children. Prince Jefri owns a coach which he uses for the children and their schoolmates. He has also acquired for them small motorbikes which they can drive around their large playroom. Jefri's house in London, in the prosperous area of Hampstead Garden Suburb, is near that of a wealthy Arab. This Arab became so incensed about the noise coming from Prince Jefri's house that he sought an injunction to stop it. But Prince Jefri did not accept the criticism of the noise-level emanating from his house and a minor feud broke out. The neighbourly animosity reached such a level that Prince Jefri ordered his coach to be started up in the mornings specifically to annoy the Arab.

Then Prince Jefri's children discovered the delights of fireworks. Not content with a modest fireworks display on 5 November, Guy Fawkes Night, they let them off whenever they felt like it. The fireworks-manufacturing company Brocks was asked whether it could provide bigger fireworks than those found in the shops. So into the grounds of Prince Jefri's house were driven four-inch cylinders much like drainpipes, which were the launchers for these 'professional' rockets.

When these fireworks were let off, some of them hurtled towards the Arab's house. The Arab, a man of some standing, thought he was under a missile attack and called the police anti-terrorist squad, which rushed to the scene. The police persuaded Prince Jefri's people to redirect the rockets so they pointed away from the house of the Arab. (This piece of diplomacy over, the police stayed to enjoy the next hour or so of whizzes and bangs.)

As well as having fun with professional fireworks in London, Prince Jefri has enjoyed them back in Brunei too. He gave a party where he entertained guests by setting off the huge rockets from their drainpipe-sized launchers. This time he could be sure there would be no problem with Arab neighbours. But the first rockets went off with such force that they tipped over the launchers: instead of facing away from the assembled guests, the launchers suddenly faced towards them. Under attack from the high-powered rockets, the guests had to run for cover.

Prince Jefri's children certainly have an adventurous time. On one occasion Prince Jefri's coach was used to ferry not only his children but also his children's classmates to Windsor Safari Park. But no sooner had the coach arrived at the Safari Park and the

The Richest Man in the World

entrance fee for all the children paid when it was decided to go somewhere completely different – Great Yarmouth, which is more than a hundred miles away. The attraction of Great Yarmouth was its amusement arcades with banks of electronic and other games. But by the time the coach arrived there, these arcades were closing for the day. Luckily one of them was found to be in the act of closing. With the aid of a £500 inducement, the arcade's operator was persuaded to keep it open a while longer. The children were then given handfuls of coins and let loose on the machines. Parents who had thought their children were out for a zoo trip and were expecting them back for supper were relieved when the children finally arrived back from Great Yarmouth at eleven p.m.

Also on the pleasure-loving side of the family is the last brother, Prince Sufri. He is close to Prince Jefri, who was the equivalent of his best man at Prince Sufri's wedding. Prince Sufri is the brother who has suffered most through the inbreeding: he has a very serious illness of the throat which makes speaking difficult. His condition has been so bad that some are surprised that he is still alive. He has been obliged to take powerful drugs which have unpleasant side-effects, including bumps all over his skin.

Perhaps because of the danger that his life may be short, Prince Sufri does not take part in government and instead pursues happiness with an engaging openness. He has been married three times (consecutively, not simultaneously) in his quest, the latest time to a Malaysian pop-singer Mazuin Hamzah. He met twenty-two-year-old Mazuin on 10 July 1987, when she came to sing at Prince Sufri's birthday celebrations in Brunei. The Prince says that when he saw the singer, 'It was love at first sight.'

Prince Sufri was happy to show his devotion to Mazuin (nick-named Awin) during their engagement. They could be seen shopping together for magazines in a bookshop in the afternoons. Prince Sufri gave her an engagement Porsche and had 'Sufri' written on one side of his own Ferrari and 'Awin' on the other.

In the context of the pretension that abounds in Brunei, Prince Sufri's unaffected enthusiasm is sea-breeze fresh. Expatriates in Brunei also admire the way he speaks in public despite his disability.

Sufri's moment of greatest prestige came in 1987 when all his brothers went to do the Haj, the pilgrimage to Mecca that all devout Muslims should make at some point in their lives if they possibly can. Sufri was left behind as 'acting Sultan'. The experiment must have been judged a success because, since then, Sufri has again been made acting Sultan. If there is a potential Emperor Claudius in the Brunei royal family, it is Sufri.

While Sufri was acting Sultan in 1987, his three brothers showed their different styles in the manner in which they did the Haj. The Sultan and Prince Jefri went together in one of the Sultan's private jets. On their return in the aeroplane, a subject of debate was what clothes they should wear for their reappearance in Brunei. A crowd was waiting at the airport and children had been lined along the road from the airport to the palace. After some differences of opinion (whether on grounds of fashion, public relations or religion remains unknown), it was decided that the Sultan and his brother should wear gorgeous Arab desert clothes. The Sultan descended in clothes of gold like a latter-day Lawrence of Arabia. His brother Jefri was draped in pale blue-grey with gold trim. Both covered their heads with black Malay caps. The attending government officials wore black Arab clothing with white Arab headdresses. The effect of this theatrical arrival of South-East Asian royalty in Arab costume was tremendous. The diplomats could hardly believe their eyes but were certainly impressed. The crowd seemed happy and crowded around the Sultan to touch him. It is considered lucky to touch someone who has just returned from the Haj, even more so if he is the Sultan.

But what of Prince Mohamed? The second brother did not return in the Sultan's private plane with his two brothers. His visit to Mecca was made on a humble commercial flight. His return was not at all an occasion for costume drama. He returned wearing very simple white clothing, traditional for Malays and Bruneians. He was without jewellery or ornament. He dressed no better than a peasant and in doing so he no doubt was expressing his humility before Allah.

The division between the two sides of the family was never more obvious. On the one side, the Sultan and Prince Jefri certainly did their Haj. But they brought to it a hint of Gucci. On the other, Prince Mohamed showed respect to his God and his country by wearing clothes both simple and local. Certainly the Sultan and Prince Jefri often wear local dress and observe local customs, but the return from the Haj was symbolic of the differences of emphasis in the family. The difference is very real and in true soap-opera style it has led to confrontation and crisis. All that was needed was something to make the tension snap. That something was the air hostess from Royal Brunei Airlines.

CHAPTER NINE

From Air Hostess to Queen

ۿ

The wish to lead out one's lover must be a tribal feeling; the wish to
be seen as loved is part of one's self-respect.
                    Elizabeth Bowen, *Death of the Heart*, 1938

The Sultan's marriage to Queen Saleha did not wholly satisfy him.
This is not surprising since she was probably as much the choice of
his father as of himself. He married her when he was only nineteen
and she sixteen. She is of royal birth and his own cousin, and she
was therefore considered suitable.

She has borne the Sultan six children: two sons and four daughters.
The sons are Al-Muhtadee Billah and Abdul Malik. The daughters
are called Rashidah Sa'adutul, Muta-Wakkilah Hayatul, Majeedah
Nuurul and Nafizah Sururul.

Queen Saleha is everywhere regarded as gentle and sweet in the
traditionally approved way for Bruneian women. However, she is
not particularly worldly or sophisticated. She was brought up
properly by Brunei standards and, as a woman, was not expected to
have much direct experience of life outside her immediate environment.

The Sultan's reputation in the late 1970s and early 1980s as a
playboy cannot have given her any pleasure. However, it must be
remembered that in Brunei it is not abnormal for men to consort
with women other than their wives. This is something that wives
are widely forced to accept. By the early 1980s the Queen had lost
her figure. Even the government-approved pictures of her which

appeared next to pictures of the Sultan in shops, hotels and offices, showed her to be very much overweight.

The Sultan's eyes roved and landed on someone very different.

In the late 1970s, the small national airline of Brunei, Royal Brunei Airlines, doubled as the private fleet for the royal family. If the Sultan wanted to go on a shopping spree in Singapore, he would ring up the airport and tell the staff to get an aeroplane ready for him. This meant that any flight for the public that was planned had to be cancelled and the plane had to be converted for the Sultan's use.

It was probably as a result of taking these flights that the Sultan came to meet and get to know an attractive young air hostess. She was a young woman who looked and behaved differently from most other Bruneian women: she was not so shy; she did not dress so often in traditional clothes; she did not cover her head so frequently; she liked parties and had an active social life; she knew something of the ways of the world.

The Sultan began an affair with her. He arranged for her to live in a house near where the Istana Nurul Iman would be built. He then helped her move to a large house in a district of Brunei called Muara. Some of the more superstitious people in Brunei said that she gave him a magic potion which enslaved him to her. The name of this bewitching woman was Mariam Bell and she was the person who would be the catalyst for a crisis in Brunei. The Sultan fell in love with her and decided to marry her. This was an affront to the tradition-minded people of Brunei, especially the Sultan's father, the dominant Seri Begawan. Most of the reasons for the antagonism towards the match lay in Mariam's background: humble, and not even wholly Bruneian.

Mariam Bell's mixed blood was a very unusual mixture. Her mother, Rashidah Saleh, was wholly Bruneian. Her father though, Jimmy Bell, was born of a British father and a Japanese mother. Jimmy Bell's father had been a British government civil servant in Labuan, an island very close to Brunei, which was a British colony at the time. So Mariam is half Bruneian, a quarter British and a quarter Japanese. As often happens when there is a mixture of races, Mariam is good looking, with long dark hair on either side of a round face.

Jimmy Bell followed his father into government employment. He became wireless operator for the post office in Brunei. Being in a Muslim country and married to a Muslim, Jimmy Bell, sometimes known as 'Dinger', converted to Islam and took a Muslim name: Abdul Aziz. Jimmy must have taken his religion quite seriously since Mariam's full name includes the phrase 'binti Haji Abdul Aziz' which means 'daughter of Abdul Aziz who did the Haj pilgrimage'.

Jimmy Bell lived in a semi-detached government house on stilts in a village or kampong called Sumbiling, not far from the capital. The house was painted with turpentine as many government houses were at that time. It turns the house black but it is cheaper than paint. Some of these old blackened houses can still be seen in Brunei. The accommodation consisted of a kitchen, a sitting-cum-dining room and two bedrooms. In this house Jimmy Bell and his wife lived in cramped conditions with their growing number of children and the children's grandmother. Mariam was the fourth child to come along. That was in 1955 or 1956. Fortunately it was at about that time that Jimmy was promoted from the post office wireless room to being chief clerk at the Customs and Excise Office, so the family was able to move to somewhat better quarters in a detached bungalow (also on stilts, as is customary in Brunei). But the bungalow was still government-owned. Jimmy Bell never owned a house of his own in his life.

Jimmy was a sporting fellow. He played billiards and soccer. He was a member of the Police and Customs Club, the 'P and C'. He liked his drink and was regarded as 'a rough diamond'. Nevertheless, he was brought up with some of the old British colonial standards of honesty in his work (which do not always apply in Brunei today).

Mariam went to school at the School of Omar Ali Saiffudien, the coeducational school named after the Sultan's father, where the Sultan himself had briefly studied. But Mariam's experience of the school was quite different from that of the Sultan. She fell among people who were not wholly sympathetic to the rule of the Sultan. For some years after Hassanal Bolkiah was made Sultan, there still seemed to be a good chance that democracy would be given its chance in Brunei. Students in Brunei were particularly interested in this possibility and some were members of the underground student movement of the People's Party.

Mariam was one of their number. She, in common with the other members, took an oath of secrecy with her hand on the Koran. This oath of secrecy was necessary because the police were on the look out for sympathizers with the People's Party. Some members of the party who had taken part in the revolt were still in jail. It is ironic that Mariam was once a junior member of a movement that wanted to remove some of the Sultan's powers. Had the movement succeeded, she would be a far less prosperous lady than she is today.

Mariam's older sisters, Nilly and Rose, became a nurse and a dental nurse respectively. Mariam also had and still has a kind, compassionate side to her nature. In a part of the world where animals are not always treated gently, Mariam saved stray cats. Her soft heart has continued into adulthood. She has a number of adopted children and supports a charity for handicapped children.

Mariam is known by many ordinary people in Brunei because she was one of their number. By the standards of Brunei women, who are trained to be quiet and obedient to their menfolk, she is vivacious and extrovert. Her clothes are in the latest fashion, which some traditional Bruneians regard as too ostentatious. Westerners, however, do not regard her as particularly outgoing or noticeable, because by Western standards she is not. By Western standards she is simply normal and pleasant.

The Sultan's romance with this charming woman was ideal for him because of his own shyness. Some people who come into contact with him were offended by the way in which he hardly managed to say hallo. They took it as the arrogance of someone who had been spoilt by too much wealth. Mariam's natural warmth and her quiet confidence were doubtless usefully complementary to him. She came from an ordinary background and yet, perhaps to his surprise, she was therefore much better equipped than he to face the world. It must have been an education and a relief. Her knowledge and experience of the ordinary world helped to put him in touch with the way other people lived. Nor was her knowledge restricted to Brunei since her parents had made her aware of Britain and Japan too. She therefore has some understanding of the world outside the hothouse atmosphere of Brunei.

Mariam's beneficial effect on the Sultan soon became apparent. One of the first ways in which she is said to have helped him is in encouraging him to play polo. The idea came from elsewhere, but she supported it. Polo helped him lose weight and trimmed him down to the fine figure that he is today. He also improved his looks later on by giving up the stubbly beard and dark glasses.

Probably more important than improving his looks, though, is Mariam's effect on the Sultan's self-confidence. He has gradually become more ready to assert himself, more poised and more at ease. But these positive results did not make the relationship any more acceptable to those who opposed it.

In the early days of the relationship, people in Brunei may not have known of the affair. Those who did know probably did not disapprove too strongly. Attitudes to mistresses in much of the Far East, including Brunei, are often different to those in the West. The Sultan's relationship with Mariam, therefore, would not have appalled Brunei society if it had continued indefinitely. The appalling thing by Brunei standards was the idea of marriage to Mariam.

Mariam was not only a commoner, but she came from a family that was not even rich or prestigious. She was merely the daughter of the chief clerk at Customs and Excise. In addition to the Seri Begawan, many ordinary people disliked the match because they felt it would demean the monarchy, which some of them hold in almost religious awe. Mariam's mixed blood was a particularly serious problem because of the Japanese element. The Seri Begawan and many other Bruneians lived through the Japanese occupation of Brunei. Many of them suffered humiliation, and the resentment often lasted their lifetimes.

There was also the fact that the Sultan was already married. Having two or more wives at the same time is not now normal for Muslims. It is perfectly legal to have up to a maximum of four, but the practice is not encouraged. The official Islamic Propaganda Organization in Brunei says that the Muslim law permitting up to four wives was framed at a time when there was a shortage of men.

Those conditions are long gone. Now only 2 per cent of married Brunei Muslim men have more than one wife. Muslim men who want a second wife are told they must question their conscience first. They have to be satisfied that they will be able to treat both wives equally. The many friends and relatives of the Sultan's first wife, Queen Saleha, were concerned that the Sultan would show preference for his new love.

With all these objections in the way, it seemed marriage was out of the question. But the Sultan's feelings for Mariam were so strong that he did not want to keep their relationship on a temporary, unconfirmed basis. Encouraged, perhaps, by the extra confidence she gave him and determined not to lose the woman he loved, the Sultan quietly, perhaps even secretly, married Mariam on 28 October 1981. (Whereas an official publication in 1985 gave the exact date of the Sultan's marriage to his first wife, the exact date of his marriage to Mariam appeared to be a mystery at that time, even to the government.) The marriage was not made public until a year later.

Sultan Hassanal's marriage to Mariam nearly cost him the throne. The Seri Begawan was furious. The marriage to Mariam may have been the most significant denial of his authority by the Sultan since the Seri Begawan put him on the throne fourteen years before. Previously the Sultan had been content to be an obedient figurehead. In private, the Seri Begawan apparently sometimes referred to Mariam as 'that Jap'. He also emphasized her common origins by also referring to her as 'Datin Mariam'. ('Datin' is a lowly title compared to the royal and aristocratic ones abundant in the top circles of Brunei.)

The Sultan had done what he wanted and he stuck to it. He now had by his side a woman whose good fortune depended entirely on him and on no one else. Mariam had every reason to want the Sultan to succeed. Such a person would be a useful friend to have on his side. But the Sultan nevertheless had to bear and bow to his father's anger.

For the first few years of the marriage, the Sultan accepted that Mariam, or Queen Mariam, should be treated as second-best of his two wives. Queen Saleha was brought onstage for official occasions, while Queen Mariam stayed at home. In this way the family rift was kept below the surface for a few years. But this could only be temporary. The marriage of the Sultan and Mariam prospered. In due course, the Sultan wanted her to emerge from the shadows. The only way for this to be possible was for the Sultan to take power for himself. He could not bring Mariam up to the rank of his first wife without a confrontation with his father. He had to meet this confrontation and win if he was to elevate her to the status he wanted. There was no way round the obstacle that his father represented. That is why the rise of Mariam and a fight for power with his father happened simultaneously. Like King Edward VIII of Britain, later the Duke of Windsor, the Sultan threatened his own throne by falling in love with a woman of whom key traditionalists disapproved.

The Sultan's fight with the most important traditionalist in his country, his father, started slowly. It surfaced at first in incidents which seemed trivial or absurd. But there is no doubt that the Sultan's power was at stake. He was risking his throne, in the famous words of the Duke of Windsor, for 'the woman I love'. The difference was that the Sultan did not accept that he should be dethroned. The difference was that the Sultan made a fight of it.

CHAPTER TEN

Battle for the Throne

———————— ᐧᐧ ————————

In private enterprises men may advance or recede, whereas they who aim at empires have no alternative between the highest success and utter downfall.

Tacitus, *Histories*, A D 104–109

The prestige and ability of the Seri Begawan were so great that an attempt by the Sultan to assume power was ambitious. The Seri Begawan had been the major post-war influence on the development of Brunei and he is referred to sometimes as 'The Father of Brunei' or 'The Architect of Brunei'. He had outwitted both the British and his own people. The Prime Minister of Singapore, the redoubtable Lee Kuan Yew, held him in such high regard that he had been known to go out to the airport and meet the Seri Begawan even when he was simply in transit there.

But the Sultan had some advantages too. The Seri Begawan's health was failing, making it obvious that the Sultan was the coming man. There was no point for ambitious men to nail their colours to the mast of a man who had suffered two heart attacks in 1981. The Seri Begawan also suffered from asthma and other ailments. He began to have two doctors in attendance so that there would always be one of them on call. The most sophisticated medical equipment was bought for him.

The Seri Begawan's mind was deteriorating together with his body. According to one report he was prone to the symptoms of a manic depressive. As he got older, he tended to become more temperamental. He would suddenly take against people and be ferociously obstinate. Meanwhile his memory was failing too.

Some of the senior Brunei government and army people were friends of the Sultan, not of his father. The Sultan played polo with people such as Brigadier-General Ibnu, his aide-de-camp, whose brother was the chief of police. The odds were in favour of the Sultan. But the Seri Begawan was still capable of a hard fight and he had the sympathy and support of many Bruneians.

In 1984, Brunei became fully independent of Britain. It was a curious event. Rare among the territories in Britain's empire, Brunei did not want to leave the embrace of the mother country. The Seri Begawan was so pleased with the protection Britain had provided for his rule that he did not want to break the bond. It was Britain which insisted.

A large number of foreign dignitaries, including President Marcos and Prince Charles, visited Brunei for the celebrations. Significantly, the Sultan was in the forefront for Brunei. The Sultan made the speeches. The Sultan even gave one or two interviews. The Sultan took the opportunity of Brunei's full independence to assert his position within government. He created a cabinet in which he himself became Prime Minister, Minister of Finance and Minister of Internal Affairs. His father was made Minister of Defence and nothing else.

These appointments need not have been important. It would still have been possible for the Seri Begawan to be the power behind the throne as before, especially if, as Minister of Defence, he could command the loyalty of the armed forces. But it gradually emerged that the appointments did mean something. The Sultan had decided that he was going to rule now, as well as reign. One early sign was that Queen Mariam was given all but equal status with Queen Saleha at the ceremonies. This was bound to offend the Seri Begawan (and indeed many others).

During the rest of the year the Sultan made a state visit to Malaysia in March, state visits to Japan and Korea in April and a state visit to Indonesia in October. The Sultan was, as it were, assuming the role which his title implied. He was also, no doubt, coming to appreciate being treated by other countries as Brunei's real head of government, instead of merely his father's puppet.

In December 1984 the Sultan made a journey that was to turn out to be particularly important. He made a sweep of the Middle East which consisted of state visits to Oman, Egypt and Jordan, in that order. And he made these state visits with Queen Mariam instead of Queen Saleha. When the state visits in the Middle East were over, the Sultan continued on to London to spend Christmas and the New Year there, still with Queen Mariam. Queen Saleha was left behind. The Seri Begawan was outraged.

While the Sultan was in London, the Seri Begawan sent a message to the Sultan that he was ill, and the Sultan must return to Brunei. The Sultan, considerably irritated, reluctantly agreed to return early and arrived back in Brunei on 28 December. It was a conflict of wills that was resolved by the Sultan giving way. The matter was kept private. But the Sultan was annoyed and the Seri Begawan was not satisfied. The ill-feeling festered for a few months, still in private.

Then in May, the Seri Begawan appeared to undermine the Sultan's position more publicly. The Seri Begawan ostentatiously showed support for another male member of the royal family, Pengiran Wadood. Wadood was the oldest son of the Seri Begawan's favourite daughter, Princess Masna. The Seri Begawan attended a number of ceremonies, the main purpose of which was to celebrate the official circumcision of Wadood. The ceremonies, according to one who attended some of them, went on for hours. Government business of importance came to a standstill because middle-ranking to senior government officials were invited and would not have dared refuse. The point of the extended ceremonies was probably to suggest to the Sultan that there were others who might be more worthy of sitting on the throne. The Sultan, it seems, was displeased. A helicopter, which a leading diplomat recognized as the Sultan's own, buzzed the building in which one of the ceremonies took place.

On 30 May 1985, the Sultan allowed the registration of a political party. The significance of this was that it was almost certainly against the wishes of the Seri Begawan. The Seri Begawan could recall all too well that the first political party established in post-war Brunei had eventually revolted against him. He had consequently been almost a prisoner in his own country. He had fought back and regained power, but he never forgot the experience and it did not endear political parties to him. The Sultan's permission for the registration of the Brunei National Democratic Party was a demonstration to his father that he would and could take major political decisions against the Seri Begawan's wishes. The Sultan was, as one diplomat put it, 'feeling his oats'.

One tactic of the Sultan was to step up the number of visits which he made around Brunei. He dropped in on villages where he would listen to grievances. He showed his good-looking face and pressed the flesh like a politician or a constitutional monarch. He also adopted the practice of appearing at mosques in different parts of the country, ostensibly going there without warning. Thus did he build up popular support.

Probably as part of the struggle, the Seri Begawan apparently made substantial gifts to all his sons – except the Sultan. This may have been intended to loosen their loyalty to the Sultan by making them more independent of him. The Seri Begawan was in a position similar to that of King Lear. He had given away his throne and now seemed to feel it had been a mistake. He felt betrayed by the one to whom he had shown favour and, like King Lear, he turned to some of his other relatives and offspring to show their loyalty to him.

Prince Mohamed, according to one diplomatic source, tried to play the role of honest broker, attempting to pacify both the Sultan and the Seri Begawan, but the Sultan apparently became disenchanted with Prince Mohamed and their relations became strained. Given his conservative views, it seems likely that Mohamed sided with the Seri Begawan. Prince Jefri, meanwhile, seemed to side with the Sultan.

On 12 July 1985 the Seri Begawan made his major move. This time there was no shadow-boxing, no room for doubt. It was a dramatic public show of conflict, making the whole country suddenly aware that there was a struggle at the top. The Seri Begawan instructed the mosques to announce at the regular Friday prayers (the most important service of the week, like the Sunday service for Christians) that he himself should be called the 'Sultan dan Yang di Pertuan' that is, 'Sultan and Supreme Ruler'. He also instructed them to call him 'Maulana', that is, 'Supreme Religious Leader'.

The announcement was tantamount to saying that he was still the ultimate boss of the country and, by implication, that his son, the Sultan, could be removed. The Sultan did not prevent the announcement being made (possibly the Seri Begawan's power in the religious community was too strong for that). But he or his officials instructed the national television company to cut short the usual coverage of the prayers. One expatriate who used to watch the prayers each Friday said that suddenly the screen just went blank. Puzzled, she turned to the radio coverage. Very soon that was stopped too. The battle was in the open at last.

Within a few days, the Seri Begawan sent an announcement to the television station in which he again referred to himself as the Supreme Ruler. The station, caught in the middle of the cross-fire, asked the Sultan's officials whether they should go ahead and use the statement. The answer came back: 'No.' The television station, which is in the control of the government and always submits to royal command, suddenly had to decide which of two conflicting royal commands to obey. The station decided to go with the son.

There were two evening-news broadcasts on the national television. The first, at seven p.m., was in English. The second, one hour later, is in Malay. In the English broadcast the reference to the Seri Begawan as 'Supreme Ruler' was omitted. The Seri Begawan must have seen this because he immediately drove down in person to the television station in the centre of the capital. There he insisted that in the Malay news the reference should be made. Moreover, he wanted the statement read out in English, as it should have been an hour before. The television executives could not oppose a command from the Seri Begawan in person. So the full statement went out. Viewers of the broadcast were astonished to find that part of the Malay news was read in English. They were even more astonished to find that the Seri Begawan, eighteen years after he had abdicated in favour of his son, was now pressing his claim to be the ultimate power in the land.

On 15 July the police force, which is armed, made a formal oath of allegiance to the Sultan. Soon after, the army also declared its loyalty to him by inserting a special prayer for the Sultan in the course of a ceremony. The Sultan was making it clear that if it came to a real fight, then he had the police and army on his side. According to one local informant, his attitude had hardened to the point where he felt, 'If my father wants to take the throne, let him try!'

This was surely the key moment. The loyalty of the army and the police force was crucial. The Sultan, it seemed, had got both.

On 27 August he again asserted his authority. He very publicly released seven political detainees, giving the men pardons, with the ceremony shown on television. These men had revolted against the Seri Begawan who had consistently refused to release them. But their release passed without any public response from the Seri Begawan. It began to look as though the old man had accepted defeat.

Then on 2 October the Sultan changed the composition of the Council of Succession. Previously the Council consisted of royals and aristocrats on the basis of their titles and positions. The Sultan changed this arrangement so that he had considerable choice in the matter of who was on the Council. Why should he make such a change? It was easy to think that he was clearing the way to put in his own men and have the son of his choice named as his successor. It was clear to those close to the royal family that the Sultan preferred his son by Queen Mariam, Prince Azim, to his son by Queen Saleha, Prince Billah. Few things could be calculated to infuriate the Seri Begawan more than the thought of a son by the part-Japanese former-commoner wife becoming Sultan of Brunei. He would also have found it an intolerable slight to Queen Saleha. The Seri Begawan became extremely agitated. But a new battle was forestalled. The Sultan smoothed the matter over by making it clear that he did in fact intend Prince Billah, the son of Queen Saleha, to be his heir. This helped to placate the Seri Begawan.

The Seri Begawan had to drop out of the battle on 9 November, when he went to London for about six weeks for medical checks. During this time, the Sultan consolidated his position further. On 13 November he released another four political detainees. More importantly, he took on the Muslim fundamentalists. On 25 November he refused to attend the Maulad, a major ceremony for Muslims, celebrating the birth of Mohammed. In an extraordinary statement, it was publicly announced on the Sultan's behalf that he was not taking part in the procession because he had not been consulted about the arrangements: 'The Sultan, as Brunei's supreme religious authority, should have been consulted but was not,' the statement said.

According to one source, what particularly annoyed the Sultan was the fact that the arrangements precluded him from going to the procession accompanied by Mariam. The procession had been divided into one for the men and another for the women. It is possible that the Sultan had wanted to use the Maulad as another opportunity to increase the public status of his second Queen. It would have been the latest in a line of such steps. First he had married her, then he had taken her on state visits in the Middle East and now he wanted to walk with her in an important religious procession.

Though he had been thwarted in presenting her in that particular ceremony, his statement was a clear warning for the future. If any Muslim official tried to dictate the way religious ceremonies were performed in Brunei from then on, he would be taking on the Sultan. Immediately afterwards, on 30 November, the Sultan exercised the religious authority that he claimed for himself. It was a small matter but one full of symbolism both for the path of religion in Brunei and for the position of women there. The women newsreaders on television stopped wearing 'tudongs', the fundamentalist-approved clothing which covers their heads. This change was made on the first day on which Pengiran Badaruddin took over as head of the radio and television broadcasting station. Pengiran Badaruddin, a humorous, worldly character, was an appointee of the Sultan.

At times the crisis took on an almost farcical aspect. There were strong rumours that the royal rift was reduced at one point to fisticuffs. More certainly true, because everyone heard it, was a bizarre public statement issued by the Seri Begawan's side, saying, as if in passing, that the Sultan had been born in a garden hut. The statement was interpreted as meaning that the Sultan should not be too proud.

The battle erratically subsided. The final result was undoubtedly a victory for the Sultan. By the end of the year he had asserted his authority over the police, the army, the media and the religious establishment. He had won all the points except for his agreement that Queen Saleha's son would inherit the throne (an agreement which anyway could later be set aside).

When the Seri Begawan returned from his visit to London after his medical treatment at the end of 1985, he was much calmer than when he had left. It was time for reconciliation. Who made the first move is not clear, but one of the friendly gestures was a gift by the Sultan to his father of a special helicopter, modelled after the one used in an American television adventure series called *Airwolf*. The inside of the Seri Begawan's 'Airwolf' helicopter was quite different, though, from the one in the series. It was equipped with the best medical equipment, making it almost a miniature flying hospital.

The Sultan made another gesture of reconciliation when he publicly kissed his father's hand at the airport as the Seri Begawan was going off on a trip. Unfortunately, the national television cameramen did not know this important event was going to happen and so they failed to film it. However, the Sultan repeated the gesture at the airport on his return and the country was thus made aware that peace had been declared.

The Seri Begawan, for his part, made a speech with a key conciliatory passage in which he said that there could only be one Sultan, clearly meaning his son. The Seri Begawan then showed himself reconciled to the elevated position of Mariam by attending a banquet hosted by her during a visit by King Hussein of Jordan in March–April 1986. The Seri Begawan even sat next to Mariam, leaving no room for doubt.

But if the Seri Begawan was reconciled, in public at least, not everyone else was. One government official emphasized in 1986 that Queen Saleha was the Queen but 'the second wife is only the second wife'. And when asked for photographs of the royal family, the government press-relations department omitted any picture of Mariam. Resistance to the elevation of the daughter of the chief clerk at Customs and Excise remained. Some could not adjust to the idea of a mere commoner becoming their Queen.

How much the conflict with his son had cost the Seri Begawan in terms of the emotional and physical drain can only be guessed. He certainly found it a disappointing end to his remarkable career, and, five months after sitting next to Mariam at the dinner for King Hussein, he died.

The Sultan was glad, at least, that he had made his peace with his father before he died. Despite the rift, despite having obtained a declaration of loyalty from the police to stop his father taking power away from him, he still loved his father and never knew it more than when his father died. The funeral was rich in Islamic and Bruneian tradition. The Seri Begawan was buried in a special mausoleum where all the rituals were observed as the electric ceiling fans whirred to give the mourners some relief from the heat. The Sultan, Prince Jefri and Prince Sufri all wore black clothing with yellow sashes. White bands were tied around their black Malay hats. Prince Mohamed was dressed mostly in white. In the Far East, white is often used as a colour for mourning and indeed all Muslims in Brunei wore white bands around their hats throughout the forty days of mourning. Non-Muslims, including expatriates, had to wear white armbands.

The Sultan and his three brothers themselves manhandled the body of their father into his grave. The four sons climbed down inside the large rectangular hole. Then the body of the Seri Begawan was brought to the edge of the grave wrapped in a gold cloth. This cloth was unwrapped to reveal a quilted blanket around the body. This too was unwrapped, leaving the body in simple white cloth like that wrapped around an Egyptian mummy. The body was passed down to the four brothers inside the grave. The whole grave and the brothers inside it were covered in a green-and-gold blanket. The four brothers took the body and laid it in a trough at the bottom of the grave. The Sultan himself adjusted his father's head so that it faced Mecca but he had some difficulty and was aided by an attendant. Once the body was in place, earth was brought in wicker baskets and laid on top of it. There was loud crying from one of the women relatives.

During the period of mourning, prayers were said every day at the mausoleum. Post-funeral prayers ('bertahlil') were also said at two of the palaces, the Istana Nurul Iman and one of the older palaces, the Istana Darussalam. All-night Koran readings and recitals of the Surah Yassin took place at both palaces.

The Sultan attended the prayers and at the end of the forty days of mourning he spoke to the nation on television. He was so distressed by the death of his father that he broke down several times during his speech and had to swallow and collect himself before continuing. It was a moving display of filial affection. But as the emotion surrounding the death of his father began to subside, the reality began to emerge: the Sultan's position now was even stronger than before. There was no one else who could stand up to him.

Thus when he came to re-shuffle his cabinet, the Sultan's favoured men moved up. Pehin Isa, a quiet bureaucrat, who had previously been kept down by the Seri Begawan, became 'special adviser' to the Sultan and Minister of Home Affairs. Major-General Ibnu, the Sultan's polo-playing companion and former aide-de-camp, became Deputy Minister of Defence (the minister being the Sultan himself). Ibnu, it appears, had not been a favourite of the Seri Begawan either.

The Sultan's consolidation of his own power was matched by a gradual increase in the prestige conferred on Queen Mariam. She appeared more often on the front page of the only national newspaper, the *Borneo Bulletin* (which is owned by the royal family). A picture of Mariam looking regal joined the pictures of the Sultan and Queen Saleha that decorated many shops and offices in Brunei. It was hard for people to ignore the fact that the Sultan tended to take Mariam with him on foreign trips. His preference was obvious, although some would rather believe or hope that there was no slight on the first Queen. They explained away his foreign trips with Mariam by saying, 'His Majesty takes Mariam because she is more experienced in dealing with foreign people.'

There was a great deal of sympathy for Queen Saleha. In October 1987 the Sultan took Mariam with him to the Commonwealth Heads of Government Conference in Vancouver. Friends of Queen Saleha gave her a birthday tea party, in part, it seemed, to show their support for her. Queen Saleha does seem a sad figure. She is quiet, modest and nice and does all that she was brought up to do. Yet she finds herself in the shadows.

Her son, Prince Billah, should have been formally announced as the heir apparent with attendant celebrations. These celebrations were planned before the end of 1987, but they did not take place. Prince Billah hardly sparkles as an ideal successor. He is a product of excessive inbreeding and perhaps also excessive privilege. One senior diplomat abruptly summed him up as a 'fat slob'. In contrast, Queen Mariam's first son, Prince Azim, is a bright-eyed, handsome child, though he, too, is said to have become spoilt.

For the time being, Prince Billah is still favourite to succeed. He is appearing at more and more official functions and is prominent among the official groups of royals and ministers who see the Sultan off on his trips abroad and welcome him back on his return. But the Sultan appears to be leaving the succession issue open. This can only worry Queen Saleha and leave Queen Mariam the hope that Prince Azim might become the next Sultan.

Meanwhile the wealth of Mariam and her family has increased. The Sultan built a palace for her (of which more later). Her brothers and sisters have all come to have lovely houses that are a far cry from the crowded government quarters into which they had been born. Her sister Rose is married to a Major Hussein who used to be in the army and then worked for Shell. He is now making a good deal of money, partly by acting for Mariam in such things as buying property.

This is something which Mariam has a penchant for. She has, for example, bought a cinema in the centre of the capital and will be redeveloping it. She is gradually accumulating a fortune in her own name. This adds to the resentment which some still feel against her. It adds to the completeness of her ascendancy.

Her victory has also been the Sultan's victory. Whereas King Edward VIII had been forced to give up his throne to marry a woman who affronted the traditionalists of Britain in the 1930s, Sultan Hassanal was able to defy the traditionalists of Brunei to make a part-Japanese commoner his Queen. The crisis was over and the Sultan had won.

CHAPTER ELEVEN

Does Money Make You Happy?

—————— ∴ ——————

Modern man's happiness consists in the thrill of looking at the shop windows, and in buying all that he can afford to buy . . .

Erich Fromm, *The Art of Loving*, 1956

Having won absolute power for himself and being in possession of the greatest fortune in the world, one of the Sultan's biggest remaining problems is which leisurely activity to indulge in next. Should he go for a whirl in one of his jet planes and then play some polo, or would it be better to play polo straightaway and then go for some shooting practice on the range? Problems, problems.

One way to understand the Sultan's lifestyle is to go through a typical day with him. From the moment he wakes up in the morning, his experiences are utterly different to those of ordinary people. As he opens his eyes, he first has to remember in which palace he has been sleeping. The Sultan spends his nights alternately in the main palace in the capital, the Istana Nurul Iman, and the new palace in the jungle, fifteen miles away, the Istana Nurulizza. In the main palace he is with his first wife, Queen Saleha. In the new palace he is with his second wife, Queen Mariam. He alternates between the two wives to fulfil his obligation as a Muslim to treat them equally.

If the Sultan awakes and finds himself with Queen Mariam in the new palace, he is likely to spend some of the morning swimming or playing tennis. If he wants to have a swim, he only has to get out of bed and walk down a gentle slope along a specially built passageway which is suspended in mid-air. At the end of the passage is a totally private swimming pool for himself and his second Queen. The pool is not merely a square rectangle surrounded by square tiles. It is a Walt Disney fantasy of a swimming pool. Large translucent stalactites hang down from above to make it seem like an underground grotto. The rest of the decoration reinforces a cool, tranquil atmosphere. But if the Sultan looks out of the large smoked-glass window he will see a totally contrasting sight of lush tropical jungle.

On mornings when he really wants to stretch himself and swim properly, he can opt instead to go to another pool in the palace, this one is Olympic sized.

After his swim he may go on to play tennis, squash or badminton.

If, on the other hand, he wakes up and finds himself at the Istana Nurul Iman with his first wife, Queen Saleha, the chances are that he will do some flying from the international airport nearby.

The Sultan has long been a qualified helicopter pilot, but he has now progressed to fixed-wing flight. He has already mastered the Gulfstream G3 and has moved on to the Boeing 727 and the Boeing 757. Naturally the interiors of the Sultan's planes are rather different from the standard. The 727 has an interior like a sitting room, with armchairs that can swivel around. The gloss of luxury even extends to the safety equipment: the buckles of the seat-belts are gold-plated.

His fleet of aeroplanes is constantly changing. In 1986 he had a Gulfstream and three Boeing 727s of two different sorts. In 1987, he had a Gulfstream, a Boeing 727 and a Boeing 757 being refurbished by Tracorp of Santa Barbara, California. An Airbus and a Boeing 767 have been to Brunei on test and it seemed possible that the Sultan might buy an Airbus. In 1988 it was confirmed that the Sultan had commissioned the D. Howard Corporation of San Antonio, Texas, to customize an Airbus A310 in utter luxury. The same company had previously customized a Boeing 747 for King Fahd, complete with elevator. The Sultan's Airbus was due in July or August 1988.

So the Sultan takes up the aeroplane of his choice and practises the most crucial parts of flying – take-off and landing. The procedure, which is common among learner pilots, is to touch down and then immediately take off again. It is heavy on fuel consumption, but that is hardly a worry for the Sultan.

If he does not feel like taking up a 727 in the morning, another way of passing the time is to do some polo practice in the grounds of the palace. Alternatively, he might go to the palace rifle-range or work out in the gym. The Sultan is tremendously fit as a result of playing so many sports.

After the hobbies, sports and games that take up much of the morning, the Sultan has lunch and then, from about 2.15 to 3.30, he is at his office in the main palace to enact his roles as Sultan, Prime Minister and Defence Minister.

Everything is presented for him by his subordinates and he usually only has to say 'yes' or 'no'. He simply sorts the papers into two piles: the 'yes' pile and the 'no' pile. It is a chairman's style of government. Unfortunately, the system is not always speedy. The pile of decisions can get quite high and sometimes it takes four months for a paper to rise to the top. When the Sultan was Finance Minister, among his other roles, foreign companies quietly complained to their embassies and high commissions about payments that were in arrears because they had not yet reached the attention of His Majesty. The foreigners were not worried about being paid (since Brunei's creditworthiness is almost unparalleled) but only about the delay in payment.

The Sultan's office routine is not inflexible. Sometimes he goes to work in the mornings as well. Then there is greater progress in reducing the pile.

The Sultan in his personal capacity can be extraordinarily prompt in paying debts. One businessman in Brunei said that the Sultan in his private business was the best payer in the royal family. A bill delivered to the palace in the morning was sometimes paid the very same day. The key thing was to send the bill when the Sultan was in Brunei and not on some foreign trip.

Sometimes other government business will need attending to. Quite often the Sultan will give an audience to an ambassador, a visiting politician or some other dignitary. The Sultan generally looks awkward or bored during these audiences and they don't last long: the normal period for an audience is ten minutes. Audiences with representatives from some countries, however, take twice as long. That is because of the need for translation when he and his visitor do not share a common language.

During these audiences the Sultan normally says very little, leaving many visitors rather perplexed and worried that they may have gone wrong. For all his growth in confidence in recent years, the Sultan is still a shy man. His most comfortable relationships seem to be with people like army sergeants or motor engineers. He seems most at ease when exchanging a few words with such people, commenting, perhaps, on the working of a machine-gun or the well-being of an injured pony. He prefers contacts where he knows his ground. Possibly he also feels less challenged by such people, who are less intellectual than the diplomats and politicians and who are willing to show him unaffected respect.

From time to time the Sultan attends the ceremonial opening of a new housing estate or a review of the army or a Koran-reading contest or some similar event. The most traditional ceremonies can be extremely slow-moving, following elaborate protocol. They require a great deal of patience. They also sometimes require special, pungent oils to be poured over hands.

The Sultan occasionally makes visits to villages where he listens to the concerns of the local people. He is good at this – not in the outgoing, cheerful way of Prince Charles, but in a quiet way. At these times he appears at his most Asian, with modesty that 'gives face' even to the most humble of Bruneians. What does not 'give face' to anyone, though, is his tendency to change arrangements at short notice. In 1986, government public-relations officials were clearly not certain when a new housing estate would be opened by him. They announced one date but then changed it to another. No one objects of course, or even considers it worthy of comment: the behaviour of the Sultan is not to be questioned.

The Sultan is accustomed to receiving humble respect from his subjects. Even the top politicians and aristocrats who line up on the tarmac of the airport to greet him on his return from foreign trips eagerly bow forward over his hand in a way that might seem overly submissive to Western eyes. When the Sultan went to Canada for the Commonwealth Heads of Government Meeting in 1987, his ministers and attendants would appear at the doorways of their rooms a few minutes before the Sultan was due to appear. At the appointed moment, an attendant would tentatively knock at the door of the Sultan's suite at the end of the corridor. The door would open a little and then open fully to reveal His Majesty, who would step forward and hand a bag with money to the attendant, who received it with a bow. Then, as the Sultan walked along the corridor, the ministers and other members of his entourage who were standing in the doorways of their rooms would bow before him as he passed by.

On Fridays, the Sultan's regime is varied because he must go to prayers. He goes publicly from time to time, but otherwise he can attend prayers in either of his two palaces, both of which have magnificent private mosques.

At some point in the afternoon he will, if he is due to see Queen Mariam at the Istana Nurulizza, hurry back there. He normally drives there, with outriders on motor bikes clearing the way for his car by blaring their sirens. If he is running late, he will fly himself back by helicopter.

With the work over for the day, the Sultan may return to one of his hobbies, sports or games. The Sultan is a fan of video games and has plenty of arcade-type machines in his palaces. When he visited Magic Mountain Amusement park in California in early 1988, he was reportedly given four guides to help him and his entourage of thirty enjoy spending thousands of dollars on the games of skill.

In the evening he can watch all his formal audiences and personal appearances on television, since they are all faithfully recorded. Anything said or done by the Sultan is invariably the first item on the news. After that comes anything said or done by other members of the royal family. Then there is domestic news, such as the outcome of a soccer match between, say, the police and army cadets. Then, finally, comes the international news.

An hour after the news comes the prime-time show. Television programmes on Brunei television reflect the royal liking for adventure series, especially American ones with fast cars or aeroplanes. The prime-time show at 8.05 each evening more often than not features such adventures. In February 1987, the weekly 8.05 line-up was: Sunday, *Houston Knight*, Monday, *T. J. Hooker*, Tuesday, *Airwolf*, Wednesday, *Rags to Riches*, Thursday, *Hunter*, Friday, *Inside Story* and Saturday, *The Flying Doctors*. Local television also showed a couple of American soap operas depicting the lives of wealthy Americans. *Falcon Crest* appeared at 10.20 on a Friday evening and *Dynasty* could be viewed at 11.00 on a Wednesday.

The pattern of the Sultan's daily life has not, of course, remained inflexible and unchanging. Close watchers of activities in the palaces have noted that polo, which the Sultan is often said to be so keen on, is in fact no longer his favourite game. One of those who has been closely involved in polo in Brunei believes that the game will die out entirely as the Sultan and his brothers get older.

The Sultan's replacement as favourite occupation in 1986 and 1987 seemed to be flying. Another game which the Sultan has come to play more of recently is badminton. This is due to the influence of Queen Mariam, who is a keen and able player herself. Golf, too, has swung into royal favour. There is already a small golf course alongside the polo club, but this is not considered adequate. The Sultan has ordered the building of a completely new, international-standard, eighteen-hole golf course to be built between the polo club and the palace built for Queen Mariam. It is hoped that international golf stars will be persuaded to play in Brunei on this superb new course. The tropical climate is terrible for growing grass, but this problem can be overcome if the ground is sufficiently pampered.

A more important problem can be the nature of golf itself. The Sultan, as became evident by his polo playing, does not like to lose. He has his own golf clubs designed and built to give him the maximum assistance, but the fact remains that golf is the most merciless of games. Even being Sultan cannot make a ball go into a hole.

Or can it? The Sultan has seen what the King of Malaysia (formerly Sultan of Johore) has resorted to in the face of golf balls that refuse to obey royal commands. The King of Malaysia was playing golf in Brunei in 1987. At one green he putted for the hole and the ball failed to drop in. The King overcame this affront by picking up the ball and putting it in.

Another technique for improving one's game is to ignore the rules. In October 1987 Prince Jefri and his son Hakkim were playing with friends around the small golf course near the polo club (the party consisted, in fact, of thirteen people, most of whom, presumably, were attendants). An expatriate club member saw one of the golfers play a ball on to the wrong green. In such circumstances the player should have picked up the ball and removed it from the green before playing it again towards the right green. However the player ignored this rule and played an approach shot directly off the green. This made a divot in the carefully maintained putting surface. The expatriate burned with outrage. He said afterwards that he thought of going up to Prince Jefri's group and telling them what he thought of their behaviour. Then he decided there were 'better ways of getting a return ticket to England'.

Meanwhile a favourite activity of the Sultan which remains much loved is soldiering. This is what he excelled at during his schooldays and he still enjoys it today. The Sultan has plenty of time to practise on his firing-ranges. He invites visiting heads of government to try their luck. When King Hussein visited Brunei in 1986, the two of them went for a helicopter trip into the jungle and fired machine-guns off at some targets. In 1987, Lee Kuan Yew, Prime Minister of Singapore, visited Brunei along with his son Brigadier-General Lee Hsien Loong. Singaporean troops train in Brunei and three of their AMX13 tanks and three M113 armoured personnel-carriers performed for the government leaders. After watching this demonstration, the leaders walked over to some Singapore-made Ultimax 100 light machine-guns at a firing range.

'Will you fire?' said the Sultan to Lee Kuan Yew.

'I'll try. I haven't fired one yet,' Lee replied.

First, the Sultan held the gun to his hip and fired long bursts, bringing down two targets about a hundred metres away.

'How's that! Both went down!' said Lee in congratulation. There was applause.

The Sultan again encouraged Lee himself to try. The Singapore Prime Minister received some hints from an army officer and also shot from the hip. After a few bursts, he too had brought down the targets.

Then his son, Brigadier-General Lee, had a go. He shot from the shoulder and missed. The protocol of the bullets was immaculate.

The Sultan's enjoyment of military hardware extends as far as Exocets. Brunei must surely be the smallest country in the world to have gone to the expense of buying those French-made missiles. Brunei is also unusual in that it indulges in the luxury of practising the firing of them. This costs over £100,000 every time.

In addition to shooting, the Sultan enjoys war games between different forces in Brunei, pitting his Gurkhas against his Bruneian forces. On one such occasion, he joined in. His side soon won.

Even when not fighting, the Sultan likes dressing up in military uniform and carrying a pistol. Queen Mariam has followed suit, so sometimes the royal couple appear at official occasions in 'his-and-hers' military costumes.

The Sultan also likes military men, starting with his Deputy Minister of Defence, Major-General Ibnu. The Major-General is close by the Sultan on many occasions, whether military or not. The Sultan's most important aide in England is a former army man, Major Hanbury. The Sultan is also on friendly terms with Lord Fanshawe, who went to Sandhurst, joined the Life Guards and then the Special Air Service (SAS). Fanshawe had contact with the Sultan when he was a junior Conservative minister in 1970–4, and he was given the Esteemed Family Order (1st Class) by Brunei in 1975.

One of the Sultan's friends in Britain has been at the very top of the military tree – becoming the Chief of Staff, no less. Field Marshal Lord Bramall is chairman of the Dorchester Hotel, which the Sultan owns. Lord Bramall was Defence Chief of Staff, the top rank in the British military, from 1982 to 1985. He knows Brunei, having served there with the Green Jackets during the 'Confrontation', when Britain fought off the Communist Indonesian threat in Borneo, and he still retains positions which keep up his connection with Brunei. He has been Colonel of the 2nd Gurkhas since 1976 and Colonel Commandant of the SAS regiment since 1985. Both the Gurkhas and the SAS are represented in Brunei – the Gurkhas publicly, the SAS discreetly.

Lord Bramall provides a very high-ranking point of contact with the British Establishment and government. He is so much a figure of the Establishment that if the trappings went any further it would be caricature. He went to Eton, he lists his first recreation in *Who's Who* as cricket (and is a member of the MCC), he is also a member of six other clubs, including the Army and Navy and Pratts, he is a trustee of the Imperial War Museum, he has been Lord-Lieutenant of Greater London since 1986, he is a Justice of the Peace and he has been awarded the Military Cross, the Order of the British Empire and the Grand Cross of the Order of the Bath. The Sultan doubtless appreciates Lord Bramall's high status and this certainly assists the British government in maintaining friendly relations with the Sultan.

One way Britain has kept the goodwill of the wealthy Sultan has naturally been by catering to his love of things military. The Sultan was invited to take the Sovereign's passing-out parade at Sandhurst in 1986. (On such occasions the Sultan is a stickler for keeping exactly to time. Unfortunately, as he was leaving the Dorchester to take the parade, one of his buttons came off. There was no time to sew it back on again so it was fixed back in place with super-glue.)

Of all the various activities of the Sultan and his family, the one that is their most common leisure pursuit, the one that shows them at their most united, the one that most simply reflects their wealth . . . is shopping.

The Sultan and most other members of the royal family are serious shoppers. One thing distinguishes the Sultan in his buying from other extremely wealthy men. He not only wants the best (which is common enough) but he is willing to pay for it. According to one of his employees who has worked for other multi-millionaires, even the super-rich usually want to cut corners. But the Sultan's attitude is unequivocal. He will pay whatever it takes.

The Sultan learned to shop early. Even when he and his brothers and sisters were children, when they came to Britain, going to the shops was the foremost entertainment. Sometimes their conscientious British nannies and minders would take them to a museum or a gallery. But Leonardo da Vinci and the antiquities of Egypt could only hold their attention for a moment. What they longed for were the beauties of Harrods and the artistry of Harvey Nichols. The shopping of the Brunei royals may not impress with its originality or elegance. But for those who are most awed by tradition, prestigious brand names, snob-appeal and expense, the Brunei royal family must rank as the greatest shoppers of the age.

The Sultan and his family shop in many places and in many ways. One of the more unusual ways takes place when they are in Brunei, but want goods from Europe. Typically, one of them leafs through a Harrods catalogue. When he sees something he likes, he marks it. He goes through the entire catalogue selecting one of this, five of that, ten in red and ten in blue. Meanwhile, another member of the family might be looking through *Vogue* magazine. She might see a dress she likes and perhaps some shoes. Quite possibly she orders five pairs of the shoes in each of the five different colours, making twenty-five pairs at a stroke. (In Brunei royal circles, the celebrated story of Mrs Imelda Marcos leaving behind 3,000 pairs of shoes when she hurriedly left the Philippines seems unremarkable.)

Once the choices have been marked, they are given to an aide. The aide rings through to one of the Sultan's houses in London, where the telephone call is taken by another aide. Notes are taken of which items are wanted from which shop. Then the aide and an assistant in London set out in a van and go to the West End. They go to some shops in, say, South Molton Street to buy some dresses, then on to Russell and Bromley shoe shop in Bond Street for some shoes and then to Harrods to pick up a miscellany of luxury articles. They then return to the van and drive to Heathrow Airport. There they deliver the batch to a flight bound for Singapore and the goods are transferred at Singapore airport on to a flight to Brunei.

Once the purchases arrive in Brunei, they are ferried to whichever palaces might be appropriate. The buyer receives his or her shoes, furniture, clothes or whatever within twenty-four hours. Of course sometimes the magazine or catalogue being rifled through is American or Italian or from some other country. In that case, delivery might take a bit longer.

If the Sultan or his family want to go out and do the shopping themselves, the equivalent for them of going to the local shops is a visit to Singapore on one of the royal aeroplanes. Queen Mariam is a keen Singapore shopper. In 1988 she was buying antique Chinese furniture there and paying with blank cheques signed by the Sultan.

London plays an important part in the Sultan's life and he does much of his shopping there. He knows London's opulent areas much better than most Londoners. Only a short walk from the Dorchester Hotel, where the Sultan usually stays, is the BMW showroom, a place which is well known to quite a few other members of the Brunei royal family and aristocracy. The purchases of BMWs and Mercedes by Bruneians are so many and valuable that they have led to a mismatch in the trade figures of Brunei and West Germany. Brunei tends to count all German cars as being imports from Germany, but Germany only counts those cars which are sold directly to Brunei, not those sold via Britain or Singapore.

The Sultan also buys German cars a little further down the road at a shop which used to be called Symbols. He bought a Porsche there in 1986. The shop sells not only custom-made luxury cars but also miniature cars for children. These cars are not the sort of miniature cars which children have to pedal along like bicycles. They are genuine cars that can be driven: the motors are about as powerful as those that drive lawnmowers. But since they are not pulling heavy lawnmowers around – only light frames – they can reach speeds of thirty miles an hour or more. They come as copies of full-size cars. Customers can buy a miniature Volkswagen Beetle, a Lamborghini or a Range Rover. In all, six well-known cars are imitated. They are manufactured in Britain and Italy and cost from £3,000 for the Beetle to £10,000 for the Lamborghini. The Sultan has bought a fleet of such cars. At the Istana Nurulizza a long row of them is lined up. The Sultan gets into them with his son by Queen Mariam, Prince Azim.

If one walks back up Park Lane and turns right up Deanery Street, one comes to South Audley Street and the delightful, old-fashioned shop, Thomas Goode and Co. Spacious and gracious, Goode has supplied china and glass by appointment to Queen Elizabeth and to many other royal families past and present. The shop still has a plate supplied to Queen Victoria and patterns shown to Tsar Alexander II of Russia in the late nineteenth century. The

Sultan, like his friend the Sultan of Oman, shops here. He buys china; 'lots of it'. It is made to order and generously decorated with gilt.

Continuing up South Audley Street, one comes to Grosvenor Square (with the American Embassy on the left) and turns right into Grosvenor Street. On the left of this street is a hairdressing and beauty salon called Geno Ventti. The Sultan seems to have such a high regard for 'Jay', a very Latin, smooth-tongued Sicilian and the senior hair-stylist, that Jay sometimes is flown out to Singapore or Brunei to do the hair of the Sultan and also that of other members of the royal family. The staff of the salon are so well liked that they get invited to the Sultan's suite in the Dorchester for parties. They are also given presents.

By patronizing Jay, the Sultan is keeping some of the profits of his expenditure in the family. Cheques payable for hairdressing at Geno Ventti used to be made out not to Geno Ventti but to a company that goes by the name of Alumgold. A search of Companies House reveals that Alumgold is jointly owned by one Giacomino Magistoro, Italian hairdresser, and Her Highness Pengiran Anak Isteri Noorhayati. Noorhayati is the Sultan's sister-in-law, the wife of his brother Prince Jefri.

The Sultan's hairdresser is one of a number of people who fly out to Brunei in order to give the Sultan exactly what he wants. The Sultan's dentist also flies out from London. He is John MacKinder, who is based in Sloane Street and who spends much of his time flying round the world attending to the molars of the super-wealthy. The Sultan's florist is Peter Travers-Clarke, who is based in Wales. He does flowers for the Dorchester, including the Sultan's suite there. As for fabrics for decorating, the Sultan uses Fabric Shop Interiors in Old Brompton Road. Fabric Shop Interiors once sent to Brunei silk material costing £200 a metre.

Returning to Mayfair and shops in walking distance of the Dorchester, if one continues from Geno Ventti along Grosvenor Street, one soon comes to New Bond Street. Turn right and New Bond Street slopes downhill. Where it flattens out, on a large corner site on the right are the double-storey windows of Asprey.

As mentioned before, Asprey is a luxury-goods shop that has

successfully used the polo strategy on the Sultan. The Sultan is one of Asprey's best customers and Jeremy Mains is the man who maintains the company's personal contact with the Sultan. Among the many items which the shop has sold to the Brunei royal family are Asprey wristwatches, which Queen Mariam gave to all the competitors in a game of badminton at her palace. Asprey won a Queens Award to Industry for Exports in 1986, which must in some part be due to the company's success with the Sultan. Jeremy Mains plays polo himself and flies out to Brunei to combine business and pleasure. True to form, Mains is an ex-army man and gets on well with the Sultan. When the Sultan is in London, Mains takes goods to the Dorchester to show to the Sultan in his suite. In fact, there is usually something of a queue of jewellers waiting in the foyer of the Dorchester when the Sultan is in London.

Meanwhile seven doors up New Bond Street from Asprey at number 153 is Van Cleef and Arpels. This jeweller has sold several items to the Sultan too. So has Cartier, which is six doors the other side of Asprey, at number 175–176 New Bond Street.

Almost opposite Cartier is a street called Burlington Gardens, which becomes Vigo Street before meeting Regent Street. A little up Regent Street on the right is the imposing façade of Garrard. This is the other jewellery house which does sufficiently well out of the Sultan to sponsor a polo match in Brunei each year. Yet, for all the prestige of Garrard as 'the Crown Jewellers' and the very many objects which traditional Asprey has sold the Sultan, these are not necessarily the jewellers at which the Sultan has spent most money.

The really expensive items in jewellery are large single stones. One very large stone is worth much more than many small stones weighing the same. The Sultan has bought for his wives some of the largest stones available. A jewel specialist at a major London auction house called the Sultan's collection of jewels 'legendary'. But the likes of Asprey and Garrard are not in the forefront of supplying these top-of-the-range gems. Another, quite different, company in a different part of London is.

Graff Diamonds is in Brompton Road between Harvey Nichols and Harrods. It is the creation of Laurence Graff, one of numerous Jewish diamond-specialists based in London. Many of these dealers have remained in their traditional base in Hatton Garden, but Laurence Graff has emerged as an international salesman of some of the biggest and most spectacular jewellery in the world. In the 1970s he prospered by catering especially to the newly wealthy Arabs with large stones and watches festooned with diamonds in an extravagance some considered gaudy and others gorgeous. In April 1988 it was Graff who won the bidding to buy the biggest diamond to be discovered in recent years. He paid a world-record price for a diamond of over US$9 million. It is Graff's specialization in the largest stones that has led the Sultan to become one of his customers.

The tremendous size of the stones acquired for the Sultan's two wives can be seen in official photographs. It is impossible accurately to value jewels from photographs since any self-respecting jeweller insists on examining them with a magnifying glass. But one official picture of Queen Mariam shows her with a diamond on her finger which appeared to a jewel expert at a leading London auction house to be about twenty-five carats. If that is correct, he would expect the diamond to be worth about US$1.5 million. In the same picture she is shown wearing oval-shaped pendant diamond earrings which are not much smaller – say the size of the top third of a little finger. These three stones are where the big money lies, and they alone are probably worth some US$2.5 million.

Meanwhile, the rest of the Queen glitters with other stones. Starting at the top, she has a diamond-studded tiara in the shape of the emblem of Brunei. The diamond earrings already mentioned hang from diamond-studded bases over the earlobes. Around her neck is a long necklace again covered with diamonds and featuring a pendant of three very large, lozenge-shaped sapphire stones. The top one is the smallest and the bottom the largest – about the size of a 50p coin.

She is wearing a yellow sash on which is pinned a brooch, also diamond-studded and again in the shape of the emblem of Brunei. At her waist she has an eight-point star of gold, silver, blue and orange. On her right wrist she wears a bracelet with more diamonds. On her third finger she wears a ring with another large sapphire, which is oblong and about three-quarters of an inch long. On her left wrist she wears a highly decorated watch with an oblong white face surrounded by what appears to be a row of sapphires inside a row of diamonds. The band similarly seems to be covered mainly in diamonds, with a line of sapphires on each outside edge. She is, in short, dripping with the most superb gemstones money can buy, and which probably cost over US$3 million, or over £2 million.

Meanwhile, Queen Saleha certainly does not let herself be outdone in her jewel collection. In a parallel official photograph she is shown with a similar tiara, even bigger pendant earrings, a necklace consisting entirely of diamonds, a brooch also consisting entirely of diamonds, a badge similar to Mariam's and a bracelet which is not so much studded with diamonds as consisting of them. This bracelet has diamonds, three across, all the way around the wrist, probably making over fifty diamonds, all of which are far bigger than those which most women have as single stones on their engagement rings. Each diamond appears to be about two carats (whereas most diamond engagement rings are less than half a carat). Her watch also has a strap with large diamonds on it. In fact, Queen Saleha's jewellery in this outfit consists almost exclusively of this expensive, clear stone.

Having taken account of the wealth of jewellery shown in these two official portraits alone, one must remember that these jewels are only a small part of the collections owned by these women. They would no more be willing to be frequently seen in the same jewels than ordinary women would want to be seen too often in the same dress.

In 1987, the Sultan was adding to the collection. He was reported to have bought a relatively small red diamond at a New York auction for US$880,000. Although it weighed less than one carat, red diamonds are extremely rare: only five are known to exist. One of the other four is in the Smithsonian Institution.

In addition to the gems owned by the Sultan's two wives, there are also lavish jewels worn by other members of the royal family, including the Sultan's sisters and his children.

The daughters of the Sultan, including one who is less than ten years old, have jewellery vastly more valuable than many a rich woman would own. Even the boys have gold necklaces from which hang rectangular blocks of gold. These blocks are so heavy that concern has been expressed that they might damage the children's spines. Even more than their father, the children are learning early about the joys of being a wealthy consumer.

Only two small blocks north of Geno Ventti is Brook Street, and another of the Sultan's haunts. In May 1986, one of the Sultan's little daughters had her birthday party in Claridges Hotel.[1] The hotel's ballroom was converted for the purpose into a mock fairground, complete with sideshows, clowns and rides. The party, for 150 children and fifty adults, had to end early because of a bomb scare. But as the children left, each child was given a camera and a ten-pound note.

For other parties given by the Sultan or one of his wives, characters from Disneyland have been specially flown over to London or Brunei to entertain his children. Such indulgences for children are not cheap. A party given for other children by the F. A. O. Schwartz toy-store which included a welcome from Pinocchio, a trip to the toy-store and a Wizard of Oz night at the Plaza Hotel reportedly cost £10,000 for fourteen children.

[1] *Daily Mail*, 13 May 1986.

CHAPTER TWELVE

Houses Fit for a King

—————— ॐ ——————

Paris Match: 'Is Adnan Khashoggi still the richest man in the world?'

Adnan Khashoggi: 'What does that phrase mean? Can one sleep in two beds at a time?'

Paris Match interview, 1986

The richest man in the world (the Sultan himself of course, certainly not Khashoggi) cannot sleep in two beds at a time, but he can get as close as possible. He sleeps in many, many different beds consecutively. His property portfolio is a stunning collection of buildings all over the world, many of them constructed or altered at vast expense to suit his taste and needs.

Some of his acquisitions have made news. His purchase of the Dorchester Hotel in London, one of Britain's top five luxury hotels, made the front pages in 1985. In the United States his purchase of the Beverly Hills Hotel made headlines for a day in 1987. Meanwhile in Singapore the Sultan's purchase of the Holiday Inn was publicly marked by renaming it The Royal Holiday Inn. And in Brunei itself, the world's press descended on the biggest palace in the world, the Istana Nurul Iman. Colour pictures of the spectacular interior appeared in magazines worldwide.

But these well publicized purchases represent nothing like the sum total of his property. He has bought other major properties that have hardly received a mention or else have successfully been kept completely secret.

In Brunei itself the most important building which has avoided substantial publicity thus far is the palace built specially for Queen

Mariam, the Istana Nurulizza. The Sultan was so annoyed about the publicity concerning the previous palace he had built, that he wanted no publicity at all for Mariam's palace. The architects and builders were made to promise to keep quiet about it. Yet it is in many ways a more attractive palace than the one which received all the hype.

The location is not far from the polo club in the Jerudong district, about fifteen miles from the capital. Driving along the sun-baked road leading to the polo club, one takes a left turning, which leads to a gatehouse with guards inside. The gatehouse has large sloping roofs with red tiles. Beyond it (and behind fencing on either side of the gatehouse) the road winds uphill to long shallow roofs of red tiles over a ridge. They look, from a distance, like an Italian or Greek mountain village. But the roofs do not cover a village; they cover the many large rooms of the new Istana.

The long roofs are designed to fend off the fierce heat of the tropical sun and they overhang so far in order to prevent the sun warming up the walls and thus the rooms inside. The building is therefore remarkably cool, even in those parts of it without air-conditioning. The informal arrangement of the building reflects a school of modern architectural philosophy: instead of the building imposing itself on the ridge, the building follows its natural contours. And where the hill descends particularly sharply, there are stilts to support the building. This makes it reminiscent of the many kampong houses of Brunei which are built on stilts in the water.

While, from afar, the building appears relaxed, unpretentious and practical, closer up the facilities and interiors are magnificent. One person who has seen much of the interior says, 'It is absolutely fabulous, absolutely lovely.'

Quite a large area of the grounds is open to the air. This part is Arab in style, with pillars rising to arches in a typically Arab shape. Just as in Moorish designs, there is plenty of shade and water and marble to keep people cool. One of the more modern features is the water rush in which the children can swirl their way down into a pool.

There is a Japanese-style garden, doubtless a choice of Queen Mariam, reflecting her part-Japanese ancestry. There is also an orchard, a running track and small zoo, which Queen Mariam sometimes invites schoolchildren to visit. The zoo is generally for her children, but it also has a special collection of birds. There are some hunting birds such as would be used by Middle Eastern sheiks for sport. Another bird of a very different sort is a mina bird, which is distinguished by its ability to say, 'Good morning' (in English) and 'God give you health' (in Arabic); it can also produce the sucking noise made before spitting (which is acceptable and traditional for many Chinese).

The sporting facilities include a total of five swimming pools, a running track, a squash court, a golf-putting balcony, a shooting range, electronic games and a badminton court. There is also the polo club less than a mile away.

The balcony putting green was something even the architect did not know about. It was a late addition, made when the Sultan began to get enthusiastic about the game. The balcony had been designed and built like any other. But then the Sultan decided he wanted to practise his putting on it and he wanted to use real turf, not a substitute. There was some doubt that the balcony would be strong enough to take the weight of the turf which was needed, but the Sultan ordered the turf to be laid anyway and, so far, the balcony is still standing.

The badminton court (blue with white markings) is for Queen Mariam. The Queen is skilful at badminton and invites teams made up of the wives of the top police and army men to play against her palace team. Though only women are present at these occasions, the players' legs are completely covered by the bottom halves of tracksuits. This is hardly ideal for playing in a tropical country, even allowing for the cooling properties of the omnipresent marble (air-conditioning is not used in the badminton courts because the air movement could affect the path of the shuttlecock). There are rows of seats for the specially invited audience, which is served non-alcoholic drinks including Coca-Cola, fruit punches and coconut milk drunk directly out of coconut shells. Afterwards they all have an ample tea together. It is a very decorous occasion.

Queen Mariam is friendly and accessible at her palace. She has not forgotten the friends of her relatively humble youth and invites them to visit her and shows them the splendour in which she is now surrounded. The electronic games are near to the badminton court. These are presumably for the Sultan or Queen Mariam (since the children were still too small to reach them when they were installed).

Prince Azim, the son of the Sultan and Queen Mariam, has his own personal suite, despite being less than five years old. It is one of the most charming parts of the whole palace, a delightful recreation of a fairytale land of knights, castles, dwarfs and little cottages hidden in the forest. Little Prince Azim can imagine himself as Sir Lancelot or Hansel or one of the seven dwarfs waiting for Snow White. The corridor leading into one room is like a path through a forest. There is a three-dimensional tree trunk with a hole that is big enough for Prince Azim to hide in. The forest path looks exactly as though it were made of stones. In fact it is a special carpet made to order in Thailand. The 'stones' are made of different colours and the pile of the carpet is cut so that it forms stone shapes.

At the end of the path is Prince Azim's dining room, which is set in open countryside. Hills and castles and a blue sky fading into the far distance are painted on the wall. Closer to hand there are some large red toadstools with white dots which are conveniently placed around a white dining table.

His sitting room is the inside of a little country cottage. Since this is a fantasy country cottage from a fairy tale, it has a tree trunk growing right through it. The chairs are giant tea cups complete with handles at the side and there is a glowing fire (which thankfully does not produce any heat). When it is time for the little Prince to go to bed, he leaves the humble cottage and goes to his castle. There he sleeps in his miniature fourposter bed, which rests on big stone slabs (another special carpet).

This suite for the little Prince is so delightful that the Thai construction workers would leave whatever part of the building they were working on and take their picnic lunch to the forest fantasyland.

In the adult parts of the palace, Arab style is mixed with traditional European. There are a large number of reception rooms. The banqueting hall is done in what one observer described as 'Austro-

Hungarian' style which is 'sort of universal for palaces these days'. The throne room is also a throwback to European grandeur of the seventeenth or eighteenth century. It may seem surprising that the Sultan has a throne room there at all, since the building is so far from the capital and he already has a huge throne room in the main palace. But one supposes a palace would not be a palace without a throne room. So there it is, with all the appropriate gilt and finery.

A large public reception room has chairs in French eighteenth-century style – that is to say, they have carved wooden frames covered in gilt with upholstered seats and backs. These come in two alternative styles: the authentic (which is elegant and uncomfortable) or the corrupt (which is the opposite).

Marble is everywhere in the palace. Nearly all the walls are covered in it. The only problem is that the new Istana, like the previous one, was built in a great hurry. The marble was not always placed with precision, so some of the walls are not completely flat.

There is one reception room that does not have a marble wall. It has wall-coverings of silk instead, with the letters 'H.B.' (standing for 'Hassanal Bolkiah') appearing repeatedly.

Gold is a theme of the palace. There is a black-and-gold jacuzzi. A collection of 'Birds of Borneo' is made of solid gold (in case anyone should doubt it, there is a notice saying, '24-carat gold'). The gold birds have wings coloured by precious stones. One is in its own special cage, also made of gold. Gold threads its way through the curtains and there is a golden coffee table – apparently solid gold, not merely gilded. It was made in Switzerland for US$2 million. There is one object which is not made of gold: a replica of the religious centre of Mecca, including the Kaaba shrine. This painstakingly crafted replica is made of silver.

The private rooms include a complete living area for the Sultan and Queen Mariam, including private access to the grotto swimming pool and the Sultan's study. The bedroom features one of Renoir's particularly luscious paintings of naked female flesh. The study was originally in the style of an English club or an English country home – quiet, dignified and traditional. The design included hardwood panelling fitted together on the spot by craftsmen from Europe. However, almost before it was finished, the design was condemned and, within six months of the palace's completion, it was ripped out. The substitute is 'all aluminium and flashing lights', in one observer's view. Another describes it as 'Star Trek' with the Sultan as Captain Kirk. It is thought that Lavia, from Rome, has been involved in the creation of the new hi-tech look. Among the gadgets is a cylindrical filing cabinet which, at the touch of a button, descends from the ceiling and automatically offers the Sultan the file he has selected. The visitors' chairs also descend from the ceiling at the touch of a button (though there was one unfortunate occasion when they became stuck halfway). Another feature of the study is a large safe containing a collection of the Sultan's impressive firearms. Also in the safe are some of Queen Mariam's extraordinary jewels.

The new palace is a comfortable place. It is less spectacular than the main one, but easier to live in. The cost was a great deal lower. Whereas the main palace is said to have cost some US$400 million, the new one cost only US$60 million for the structure and probably about the same again for the decor, furniture and *objets d'art* – a total of US$120 million. The architect was a Brunei national called Ibrahim, who trained at the Thames Polytechnic in Hammersmith, London, and runs a modest local architectural practice.

But Mariam's palace, like the Istana Nurul Iman, never stays the same for long. The fairytale suite for Prince Azim has been ripped out because the Prince wants something bigger and more adult. A huge new reception room has been reconstructed so that Queen Mariam can welcome large numbers of guests on the Muslim day of Hari Raya, when everyone must be made welcome. This enlarged reception room will enable her to compete better with Queen Saleha, whose palace was designed especially with such ceremonial occasions in mind. The style of the constantly changing rooms is not getting better. The hi-tech study apart, it is becoming, one insider says, 'flashier and more florid, more "Louis Farouk"'. ('Louis Farouk' is the derogatory name given by design professionals to the ornate style created by Arabs when adapting antique French designs.)

In London the Sultan has normally stayed at the Dorchester, although he has other properties there (of which more later). The Sultan previously tried out a number of the top luxury hotels on his visits to London but found he kept coming back to the Dorchester.

One of London's top five hotels, the Dorchester is about two-thirds of the way down Park Lane, built on the site of a house once owned by the 3rd Marquess of Hertford, one of the four richest men in England. Work began on the Dorchester Hotel at the end of 1929. The interior design was meant to be 'as nearly as possible on the same lines as the best class of English private house'. Among the special features were 'a ladies' Turkish Baths with gymnasium, beauty parlour, slimming rooms and hairdressing rooms, which will contain all the best known forms of baths, such as Vichy baths, wax baths, foam baths and the rest.'

In the years before and after the Second World War, the Dorchester became fashionable in high society. Queen Elizabeth, when still a Princess, attended her first public dance in aid of charity there. Her engagement to Prince Philip was announced when she was attending a dinner at the Dorchester and Prince Philip had his stag party there. The hotel has often been used by visiting heads of state to give banquets for the Queen in return for banquets she has given them in Buckingham Palace or Windsor Castle. King Hussein of Jordan, President Ayub Khan of Pakistan and King Faisal of Saudi Arabia are among those who have used it for the purpose. So, too, is the Sultan of Brunei.

A decline in the standard of the furnishings during the 1970s was arrested in the early 1980s when two Arab consortiums in succession owned the hotel and renovated some of the public areas. The most distinctive part of the hotel is a long, wide, high-ceilinged promenade in which people have afternoon tea. This promenade was embellished with Roman columns and generous amounts of gold leaf. The foyer was decorated with even more gold leaf. Somewhat incongruously, the bar was redecorated to look like any other hotel bar anywhere in the world. Many of the bedrooms and bathrooms, however, were not renovated at all and offered declining English gentility rather than Middle Eastern, English or any other kind of opulence.

Still, the Sultan was attached to the hotel and his main difficulty was that if he came to London unexpectedly his suite might already be booked. This problem was part of the reason why at the beginning of 1985, the Sultan bought the Dorchester outright, paying a sum variously reported to be £43 million, £50 million, £80 million or more. Having bought the hotel, he could have his suite whenever he wanted it. The Sultan let it be known that he was ready to spend £20 million to improve the hotel. On the surface, however, it did not seem as if changes costing anything like as much were actually made until more than three years later.

The Sultan's private suite, to which he was so anxious to obtain permanent access, was on two floors. The lift took a visitor to the eighth floor of the hotel where, if the Sultan was in residence, he was met by two powerful-looking security men. There were other rooms on the same floor, so the Sultan's suite had a special lobby. This lobby had a video camera which relayed a picture of the visitor to the Sultan in his study. If the visitor gained access, he found a suite that was divided into two floors and styles. On the eighth floor the reception rooms had been redecorated by previous Arab owners to include such elements as carpets with lurex thread. The style, according to one English visitor, was 'really naff'. Another called it 'ghastly'.

A mirrored staircase led up to the ninth floor, which was quite different. This upper floor contains the bedroom, bathroom and dressing room. This had not been redecorated and still had wood panelling and oil paintings. Though a little frayed at the edges, the rooms had charm. The pictures included ones of the Sultan and his father. In fact, the whole suite was named after his father. But the pictures also included some described as 'horrendous' and, 'much like the cheap paintings on sale along the railings in London's Bayswater Road at the weekend'. They included a very wide picture of the back of a reclining nude described as 'awful'. Among the best features of the upper floor were the large picture windows that went down to the floor and provided lovely views across Hyde Park. These windows could easily be seen from Park Lane.

The Sultan himself ventured out into Hyde Park while staying at the Dorchester, to go jogging in the mornings. He then ate kippers for breakfast. He and his entourage, who occupied the entire eighth floor when the Sultan was staying, also ate a great deal of Chinese food. A Chinese cook was especially brought in to prepare the food which cost some £60 to £70 per meal, excluding drinks. The high cost of these meals did not please all the entourage, some of whom had to pay the bills out of their own pockets. Part of the explanation for the cost was that some of the ingredients were bought from the luxury store, Harrods.

A recent enthusiasm of the Sultan's is playing snooker. He had a snooker table installed for his use on the hotel's mezzanine floor near the corporate offices. In the spring of 1988, his oldest son, Prince Billah, had a series of snooker lessons on this table. The top players in the world, including Steve Davis, Dennis Taylor and Terry Griffiths, gave him tips for a reported £3,000 per lesson.

The Sultan often dressed quite casually while staying at the Dorchester, and was sometimes to be seen in jeans and a sweater. Some of the staff didn't even recognize him. But others remember him well because he gave cash tips of hundreds of pounds at a time.

The management certainly tried hard to look after the Sultan while he was there. In January 1988 he was staying at the Dorchester and visiting the Casanova casino near Grosvenor Square. A line of limousines ferried him and his entourage there in the afternoons. At one point he was reputedly £2 million up, but then he lost it again and more besides. This information was splashed across Nigel Dempster's gossip column of the *Daily Mail* on 21 January. The manager of the Casanova was appalled when he saw the item and immediately rang the Dorchester asking to speak to the Sultan to apologize that His Majesty's gaming habits had been revealed. The Sultan is notoriously difficult to reach and it seems the manager did not get through. However the management swiftly reacted to the call. They removed every single copy of the *Daily Mail* that they could find from the hotel, so that the Sultan should not be upset by it.

The Sultan's early plans for large scale refurbishment did not take place immediately after he bought the hotel. But in early 1988 he announced that it would close at the end of the year for extensive works. That means he now has to stay elsewhere in London. He does not lack choice. In addition to the Dorchester, the Sultan has a number of other properties in London which have never been written about. Two of them are outstanding.

The largest one is a house 20 minutes' drive west of central London, in Southall. This is not a smart part of London: the shops overflow with saris and spices; there are men with long white beards and traditional white costumes; the food, the clothes, the faces, the music and the language all come from the Indian sub-continent. It is a comfortable place, inhabited by relatively successful immigrants and their succeeding generations.

The Asian community of Southall is probably unaware of the nearby presence of their fellow Asian. The Sultan's home is on the outskirts, near where the district joins with the middle-class surburb of Osterley. The grounds of the house are actually adjacent to those of Osterley House, the historic building owned by the National Trust and open to visitors. The Sultan's house is fronted by one very long wall along Windmill Lane. Driving alongside it, one hardly notices that one is passing anything at all. The long wall, if it suggests anything, brings to mind some institution like a hospital or school. There is an entrance where the wall dips in towards a solid double gate. On the left is a metal microphone/speaker set into the wall. On the right, also set into the wall, is a rectangle of one-way glass. The Sultan's security men can see you, but you can't see them. That is all. There is no name-plate, no number, no sign of any kind. The security and anonymity are total. The perimeter of the pro-perty, where it is not defined by the brick wall, is protected by a high wire fence with barbed wire on top.

Inside all this protection was once a restrained, fairly elegant cream-coloured stucco house. The house was known as the 'Aviary' although some maps of London have it marked as 'Woodlake'. It has extensive grounds, half a mile wide from east to west; in all, some forty-seven acres. The grounds at the east end are bisected by the M4 motorway.

The previous owner was an elderly lady who did not want the aviary she kept there torn down by her successor. Nor did she want the house to be torn down and replaced by a new housing estate. Furthermore, she wanted her faithful retainers to be faithfully retained. This was all a bit much to ask of Barratt's the house-building company which was willing to pay £3 million for the property. They wanted to take advantage of the large amount of land to build plenty of new houses. The old lady held out against the temptation of £3 million, hoping that someone else would buy it who was willing to keep to her conditions. For some time, nobody could be found who would pay a price in the same league. Then the

Sultan offered to pay £1.3 million and agreed to keep to her conditions. Fortunately, the keeping of birds is one of the Sultan's own hobbies anyway. The elderly lady accepted his offer.

However, the Sultan did want to make a few changes. And then he wanted some more and then more again. In fact ever since the Sultan bought the house there has been so much replanning and rebuilding that he has hardly had a chance actually to use the house. That is why he stays at the Dorchester. In his development of the Aviary, the Sultan has taken one of the biggest pieces of undeveloped land in Greater London and set about turning it into the grounds of a new palace. Whereas elsewhere in Britain large stately homes are falling apart, in the surprising environment of Southall, the Sultan is creating a beautiful new one.

He started modestly. In 1981 he applied for and got planning permission to build a squash court. In the same year he applied for planning permission for alterations to the outbuildings. Then he wanted to raise the height of the boundary wall, erect a gatehouse and create offices where the old aviary had been (the aviary was moved to another part of the grounds near the wall against Windmill Lane). This was enough for a while. But in early 1985, after a year in which he had increasingly been taking power for himself back in Brunei, he decided on even bigger improvements. Everything was made larger and grander. The two pillars on either side of the front door were replaced by ten pillars which supported a *porte-cochère* (a roof to protect cars stopping immediately outside the front door). The front door itself was enlarged and set forward. The front hall was enlarged. Two rooms facing the garden were knocked together and also extended back into a large bay, the whole width of the room. The other two rooms at the back, the study and the dining room, were both given new symmetrical bay windows. A muddle of small rooms was knocked out to create an elegant octagonal hall. The kitchen was enlarged, a laundry room was created nearby. A jacuzzi was added alongside the indoor swimming pool. It was set in a specially created semicircle of darkened glass so that His Majesty could sit in his jacuzzi and gaze out at his garden without any fear of being seen himself. Over the swimming pool a new first-storey wing was added, with new bedrooms. A new staircase was added so that the Sultan could descend directly from his bedroom to the indoor swimming pool. Hardly a room in the house was left un-altered. Floor levels were changed, new units, cupboards, lavatories and bathrooms put in. New windows were added and old windows bricked up. Walls were moved a yard here or there or else removed and replaced.

Meanwhile, on the outside the change in look made by a hundred small alterations created a major change in appearance. The Ealing Council town planners, when they assessed the original proposal, commented: 'The various alterations and extensions will alter the appearance of the building from what appears at the front as an imprepossessing [*sic*] flat-roofed building to a building with a mock-Georgian character. The various works are considered satisfactory and should provide a building more appropriate to its impressive setting.'

In April the same year, John Barnes and Partners of Tonbridge, Kent, applied on behalf of the Sultan for permission to erect security fencing 'in order to protect the estate in view of its owner's known wealth. Further, there is a rare collection of birds which require protection.' The black plastic-coated chain link fencing would be three metres high with three strands of galvanized barbed wire.

Then in June the same year, Major Hanbury, the Sultan's aide in Britain, applied for improvements to his offices, which were located among the outbuildings. He also applied for a new octagonal summerhouse with a diameter of six metres. In December, yet more planning permission was sought, this time for four double gates for access to the property.

Having sought and obtained all these planning permissions, an ordinary man might have been satisfied and his bank account emptied. But the Sultan soon scrapped the major rebuilding and in June 1986 started all over again.

He instituted a brand new and even bigger rebuilding pro-gramme. The walls would be moved again. The fittings replaced again. The rooms made bigger and more numerous. New facilities would be introduced. A large new wing of the house was to be built and a new storey and new staff accommodation and new security provisions would be added.

After these wholesale alterations and extensions, what sort of house will the Sultan have? After entering by one or other of the new double gates which lead to the house, the visitor will come to the *porte-cochère* (as per the first rebuilding). Passing through the front double doors, the visitor will find a marble-floored 'entrance area' with two wide symmetrical staircases winding up to the first floor. The 'entrance area' has a very high ceiling, which rises up to the roof of the house at the top of the second floor. Directly ahead of the front door are double doors to a carpeted foyer with two three-seater sofas and a fireplace to the left and occasional seating and tables on the right.

Walking further on in a direct line from the front door the visitor finds two semi-circular steps up to a marble-floored drawing room which is thirty-two feet wide and thirty-six feet long. It has three french windows opening on to the garden. Through double doors to the right is a thirty-two-foot-long dining room. To the left is the Sultan's study with two more french windows. From his study he can walk up a few steps to a television room with a built-in semi-circular sofa. Immediately next door is a small 'museum'. Beyond this, in the east wing, is the indoor swimming pool with jacuzzi, sauna and changing rooms.

The west side of the house, very much enlarged, now has a lobby, adjoining the dining room, with a marble floor arranged in geometric patterns. Nearby is a pantry and a very large kitchen to serve the main dining room and also a separate dining and sitting room for the royal entourage. The west side of the ground floor also includes a storeroom, three double bedrooms all with bathrooms en suite, a laundry room, a staff sitting room and a bedroom for the 'duty cook'.

On the first floor, the double staircase leads to a large landing and then up a few steps to a wide corridor. This leads to double doors and another sitting room. This is the Sultan's private sitting room, which is thirty-two feet wide and has three french windows leading on to a balcony the full width of the sitting room. The sitting room has Roman pillars which are echoed by more pillars on the balcony. The sitting-room ceiling is high on the side nearest the windows, where it rises up into the space of the new second floor.

Branching off from this private sitting room are two master

bedrooms which similarly rise into the second floor. Why the Sultan specified two master bedrooms is unknown. Perhaps the second is for visiting dignitaries of equal status to the Sultan. One source suggests that the Sultan and Queen Mariam like to move around to different bedrooms in the Istana Nurulizza. They stay together but they like a change of scene. If they do that at the Istana Nurulizza, perhaps they would also like to do it at their Southall mansion. Both the master bedrooms have very large dressing rooms en suite and, of course, large private bathrooms. The bathroom on the east side has an Arabic theme and a so-called 'environmental bath' (exactly what an environmental bath is remains a mystery). This is in addition to the usual facilities, including showers and bidets. The dressing room has built-in cupboards thirty-four feet long. There is a private staircase descending towards the swimming pool on the ground floor. The bedroom on the west side has yet more Roman pillars. The huge dressing room has built-in cupboards extending forty-three feet. Its bathroom has a large jacuzzi. The lavatory and bidet are conveniently placed in a separate room within the bathroom (presumably to enable two people to use the different facilities of a bathroom at the same time). The master bedroom on the west side has the further advantage of a spiral staircase rising from the dressing room to a gymnasium on the second floor. Nearby the gymnasium there is a sauna and a hairdressing room.

In addition to the two master bedrooms, the first floor also has six other bedrooms, all with bathrooms en suite. There is also a 'family room' with television and a very large and high playroom which also rises into the space of the second floor. This playroom houses a large model spaceship which a child can climb into. The spaceship is so big that it extends up to the second-floor space, which can otherwise be reached by a spiral staircase within the playroom. The rest of the second floor contains two storerooms and a plant room.

The house's appearance on the outside is more French than British, with a distinct classical influence. The pillars in the centre, both front and back, enforce the classical aspect. The ranks of evenly spaced windows, the ironwork over some of the roof, the balustrades and architectural detail like stone vases are reminiscent of French classicism. The house is impressive because it is at the top of a slope

The Sultan plays many games, from polo to pinball, but perhaps his favourite game is playing soldiers.

Though overawed by his father in his youth, the Sultan later struggled with him for ultimate power in Brunei.

Chandeliers weighing a ton each hang from the computer-designed roof of the massive throne room in the Istana Nurul Iman – the biggest palace in the world.

Two miles away, the wooden walkways of the water village Kampong Ayer are propped up on stilts above untreated sewage.

ne people feel sorry for Queen
eha, the Sultan's first wife, because
Sultan also took a second wife –
ich is his right under Islamic law.

In marrying Queen Mariam, a part-
British, part-Japanese former air-
hostess, the Sultan infuriated his
father.

Once the leading businessman in the Philippines, polo-playing Enrique Zobel built the biggest palace in the world.

The Sultan bought the Dorchester Hotel in London because he liked to have the best suite constantly at his disposal. In late 1988 he closed it down for extensive refurbishment.

Prince Billah, the oldest son of the Sultan, takes a snooker lesson in the Dorchester from Terry Griffiths – one of several top players to teach him at £3,000 per lesson.

Protected from anything short of a tank attack, the Sultan's newly built stately home in London comes complete with tennis court, badminton court, a two-storey playroom, stables, lake and exotic birds.

Mohamed Al-Fayed, social mountaineer, reaches the Prince and Princess of Wales.

Al-Fayed is less at ease with Edna Everage at the opening of Harrods sale – Harrods is the flagship of the stores group he bought in 1985.

Two of the Sultan's sometime friends, Adnan Khashoggi (international arms dealer, *left*) and the Swami (worldly spiritual adviser – bearded) with the Swami's assistant, known as Mamaji (*right*), and 'Tiny' Rowland. At various times, these men were all in conflict with Al-Fayed.

The Sultan with his sometime spiritual adviser, the Swami (shaven in this photograph). The woman appears to be Queen Mariam.

Khoo Teck Puat's austere appearance disguises a business maverick. The Sultan discovered his unorthodox activities and issued a warrant for his arrest.

When in Brunei, do as the Sultan does. Lee Kuan Yew, Prime Minister of Singapore, uncharacteristically shoots from the hip while the Sultan watches from the extreme left.

which descends down to the lake. After the latest additions the house will also impress because of its size: the width will be sixty-two yards and the depth twenty-five yards.

As well as the house itself, there are numerous other facilities and buildings. Leaving the drawing room through the french windows one comes to a wide terrace that leads down some steps to a circular fountain with curved benches at either side. The lawn continues the slope down towards a long lake that runs parallel to the house and extends right across the whole of the land attached to the property, even under the M4 motorway. The lake has a fountain in the middle and, to the west, a heron sculpture.

An open-air swimming pool lies between the east wing and the lake, together with changing and shower facilities. Further east across the lawn is the boathouse at the lake edge, with attached squash court. Just behind this is the badminton court. Permission was applied for this soon after Queen Mariam came to London to inspect work in progress in early 1987. The badminton court has a touch of Brighton pier about it, combining a greenhouse effect with some eastern designs, such as roof corners which turn upwards. Queen Mariam and the Sultan are able to play badminton there in natural light because of all the glass. They can also sauna and shower before they leave. Next door to the badminton court is a tennis court. Walking back towards the house on the pathway next to the wall against Windmill Lane, a visitor passes the tropical house and the greenhouse on the right.

Crossing to the west side of the house, next to the fountain in the garden, there is a formal rose garden that leads up some steps to the domed, octagonal summerhouse. This leads in turn to a bar and a sunroom. On the other side of the sunroom is a courtyard with pillars, in the middle of which is an open-air spa bath (which has jets of hot, softened water). The spa bath is quite secluded, with trees in front (which are in the horses' paddock) and the new aviary to the side. There are separate changing rooms for men and women.

These outbuildings again have a flavour of Brighton pier. The new aviary in particular has much elegant glazing of a sort that might come straight out of the Regency period. The pillars and the balustrades repeat the classical theme.

As for the buildings which provide the service back-up to the operations of the house, they are prodigious. There is an office for Major Hanbury, his assistant and two secretaries. There is a barn, farm buildings, hay store, stables, garages, a canteen block, a vehicle workshop, a security wing with accommodation for seven and further staff accommodation for another eight people. The staff have a lounge, a dining room and a special dining room/lounge for female staff only. The security staff have their own day room and of course a security control room with television screens showing the pictures transmitted from video cameras in and around the main house. The control room also has direct view of the main entrance of the house. The location of the Sultan's three safes in the house could also be mentioned but, in the interests of his security, they are not.

The house has some practical advantages. It is exactly equidistant between Heathrow Airport and West Kensington. Since the Sultan generally visits England for relatively short stays of between one and six weeks, the proximity to both the airport used by his national airline and the facilities of central London is very convenient. But these advantages have drawbacks attached. The reason it is so convenient for both London and Heathrow is that the house is on the motorway. And above the motorway is the flight path into Heathrow airport. So every minute or two a jet airliner cruises overhead, making a noise that can't be missed. Still, since the Sultan enjoys flying aeroplanes, perhaps he enjoys watching and listening to them too.

The second remarkable building that the Sultan owns in London is outstanding in the first place because of its location: number 20 Kensington Palace Gardens. Kensington Palace Gardens is the most extraordinary street in London. Running in a straight line from Notting Hill Gate to High Street Kensington, it is not so much a street as a gracious avenue with mature trees on both sides. The unusual nature of the street is immediately obvious, because despite being in the very centre of London there is hardly any traffic. Every now and again a car will arrive or depart, but there is no through traffic at all because at either end of this avenue are gatehouses manned by policemen. Before cars are allowed to enter, the occupants have to explain themselves. Pedestrians are allowed in freely but not many pass along the quiet pavements, which offer no shops, banks, building societies or stations. What they do offer, in plenty, are embassies. Kensington Palace Gardens is a private avenue of embassies. It used to be called 'millionaire's row' when the grand houses there were in private hands, but now the houses are well out of the reach of mere millionaires. Only countries can afford them: countries and the Sultan of Brunei.

In fact, there are still one or two other houses in private hands. King Fahd of Saudi Arabia bought the house opposite that of the Sultan – number 12. He had it fitted with a discothèque, among other things. But he is believed to have passed it on to a sister. As for British citizens who own houses in the avenue, there are none. The electoral register shows only a few British residents apart from staff, and, even these few are in houses that have been divided into apartments.

So the neighbours of the Sultan in this, the most exclusive street in London, are embassies, including those of the Soviet Union, Israel, Nepal, the Netherlands, Kuwait and the Philippines. The policemen walking up and down the pavements are from the diplomatic section of the force and are often armed. The Sultan's other neighbours are the Prince of Wales and members of the British royal family, who live at Kensington Palace, set slightly away from the avenue at the south end. The houses are solid, grandiose statements of wealth and many of them, including the Sultan's, are Victorian. The Sultan, true to form, is having his house completely refurbished and rebuilt. In fact, it seems his original idea was to demolish the existing house completely and start again, but he was dissuaded from this. Instead, he is making changes which are a true sign of extreme wealth: removing extensions and alterations made by previous owners. He is making the house smaller, in order to restore it to its original size and symmetry.

In doing so, he is pleasing the Historic Buildings and Monuments Commission which argued that the restoration work should 'follow authentically the original form as shown in the Bedford Lemere photographs taken in 1893 (National Monuments Record photographs numbers 12/221–9)'. The director of planning at Kensington and Chelsea Council wrote to the Department of the Environment that 'the proposal has the full support of English Heritage and the Victorian Society and it does, in my view, represent a significant gain in conservation terms'. The solid Victorian design is not Victorian Gothic and bears no relation to most Victorian residential architecture. Instead it is in classic style with Roman pillars.

The interior, of course, does not have to be Victorian and it is not. The Sultan's liking for marble floors is evident and all four large rooms on the ground floor have geometric-pattern marble floors. All the rooms – reception room, drawing room, study and dining room – have fireplaces. The reception room, which is on the left of the house as one faces it, is the biggest room, measuring thirty by twenty-five feet. The dining room has four pillars – clearly one of the Sultan's favourite design features.

The Sultan's master bedroom has been hacked out of several rooms. It is on the right side of the front of the house as one looks from the street and it stretches thirty-five feet across, taking it beyond the middle of the house. The rest of the front of the house on the first floor is taken up with a 'closet', or dressing room, containing nothing but built-in cupboards for the clothes of the Sultan and whichever wife may be with him. There are even a couple of clothes cupboards back to back sticking out into the room, rather like bookshelves in a library. The total length of the built-in cupboards is thirty-two feet. The Sultan's bathroom is next door and can be reached from the closet or from the bedroom direct. It has the unusual feature of two lavatories side by side, each in its own cubicle. The rest of the floor is taken up with another study and another bedroom with en suite bathroom. The second (and top) floor has a further four bedrooms with en suite bathrooms. Meanwhile, at the bottom of the house, the lower ground floor or basement has the kitchen, 'control room' (for security), staff accommodation and some of the Sultan's usual facilities: a swimming pool, gymnasium, sauna and a second pool.

The house also contains two lifts – one a goods lift and the other for the Sultan. The house has another safe but, again, its whereabouts will not be mentioned here. The security systems, incidentally, will doubtless be as elaborate as at the Aviary. Even while the house was little more than a building site, a company called Apollo was handling security.

In addition to the Dorchester, the Aviary and 20 Kensington Palace Gardens, the Sultan also owns a house in Hampstead in Reddington Road. He has owned this house for many years and it is used by staff and various members of the royal family when they are visiting London. The Sultan has also bought a house in the road which is the present 'millionaire's row' of London, Bishop's Avenue, another wide, tree-lined avenue, this one not far from Hampstead Heath and the stately home of Kenwood. This road is quite unlike most London roads and more like a street in Beverly Hills. All the houses are very large, detached and with gardens of about an acre each. The Sultan is thought to have given this house to one of the female members of his family.

This part of Hampstead, known as Hampstead Garden Suburb, has clearly been a favourite spot for the Brunei royal family and they almost certainly own a number of other houses in the neighbourhood. Prince Jefri owns a house in Winnington Road, which is parallel and of similar status. It is a broad road that glides down a curving incline. There are no cars parked in the street: they are all in large garages and huge drives. When one can see any car at all it tends to be a Rolls-Royce or a large Mercedes. The street is unnaturally tidy and quiet. The atmosphere is surreal because of the lack of people. The owners seem to travel only by car and anyway much of the time they are in other homes they own elsewhere in the world. It is an area where Arabs and Jews live together. They are very security conscious: one person who parked in the street to look around noticed a man wearing a Jewish skullcap surreptitiously emerging and taking a picture of him before scurrying off again.

Prince Jefri's house is number 37. His wife Princess Noorhayati spends much of her time in London. They have one of the very few vehicles parked in the street: a smart blue Mercedes coach which can carry about twenty people. A security man approaches anyone who takes too close an interest.

Other properties in Britain of which only little is known are another house owned by the Sultan, this time in the St John's Wood area. Queen Mariam also has a house or flat near Sloane Square, and one of the Sultan's sons has also had property which has been bought for him. Doubtless the Sultan and the family have other properties in London too. Some of these are investments rather than homes; perhaps they are also a form of insurance. If the royal family is ever forced to leave Brunei and want to settle in Britain, they will certainly not be short of places to stay.

The Sultan also has a range of boltholes outside Britain. In California he owns the Beverly Hills Hotel, Los Angeles. This prestigious hotel, also known as the 'Pink Palace' because of its colour theme, is frequented by Hollywood stars and its Polo Lounge is a popular breakfast place for people in the film industry. The hotel has 260 rooms and 'cottages'. The Sultan bought it through a company called Sajahtera in September 1987 for a sum reportedly over US$200 million. That means that the price per room was US$770,000, which was a record price at that time. (It has since been broken by the Japanese.)

The Sultan bought the hotel from oil tycoon Marvin Davis, who in turn had bought the hotel from the family of disgraced financier Ivan Boesky for about US$135 million. It seems that the Sultan was the underbidder when the Boesky family sold out, but he continued to pursue the 'Pink Palace' afterwards, eventually offering Davis such a big profit in under a year (US$65 million) that he could not resist it. Davis was also encouraged to sell by the cost of refurbishing the hotel. The Sultan was said to be ready to embark on a US$40 million renovation of the hotel, although by February 1988 there was still little sign of this taking place.

The Sultan also reportedly bought three of the finest residences in Beverly Hills in early 1988 for a total of US$15 million. His intention was apparently to knock them down and rebuild. One of the best houses was owned by James Coburn's ex-wife. The Sultan wanted to demolish it and replace it with a mini-palace of some 65,000 to 100,000 square feet.

In Singapore, the Sultan has bought two hotels, of which he has since sold one. He had often used the Brunei Suite in the Goodwood Park Hotel, which was owned by one of his advisers, Khoo Teck Puat. But the Sultan developed a desire to have the luxury suite constantly available to him. The only problem was that he sometimes arrived without giving more than two hours' notice. This could cause problems in 'personalizing' the suite in time for his arrival, quite apart from the fact that the suite might at that time be already occupied.

The answer to the problem was to buy the Holiday Inn in Singapore, which also happened to be owned by the family of Khoo Teck Puat, and in August 1983 he did, for a reported figure of Singapore $250 million. Renamed the Royal Holiday Inn, it is in the same street as the Goodwood Park, but on the other side. It is a bustling hotel and much less smart than the Goodwood Park. The Sultan began by using the penthouse, but he soon tired of travelling so far by lift, so he moved to a lower floor. He did not take merely a suite, he took the entire floor and had it reorganized to his liking, with the installation of a whirlpool. The management of the hotel, like any professional management, would have liked to rent out the enlarged suite to other guests while the Sultan was away, but the Sultan declined permission. While he was away the door was kept locked.

The door, though, was not where one might have thought. The Sultan was not keen to parade himself and his companions through the busy lobby of the hotel. It so happened that next door to the hotel was a car park. He bought that too and arranged a passageway from the car park directly to his suite. There were other passages between the two structures, but this passageway was exclusively for access to the Sultan's floor. The simple, painted door was in the corner of the parking area on the equivalent floor. The door was and remains completely unmarked. There is nothing to indicate its purpose. But there is a clue to the fact that it is an entrance to someone who is security conscious. Just to the right of the door is a metal-fronted entryphone.

Having bought the hotel in 1983 at the peak of the Singapore cycle in hotel prices, by 1986 he had tired of it. He sold it when hotel prices were depressed. But he managed not to sell at a loss. He sold it to the Brunei Investment Agency. Meanwhile he bought another hotel just across the road – the Singapore Hyatt. He paid Singapore $183.48 million (equivalent to US$84.4 million at the time) in September 1986. The Hyatt in Singapore is an ultra-modern hotel with a vast open reception area covered in marble flooring. The Sultan once again had a suite especially renovated for his personal use, and he incorporated some of the furnishings that had previously been used in the luxurious Hugo's Restaurant within the hotel.

In Malaysia the Sultan bought yet another property. This was a mansion on Ampang Road in Kuala Lumpur. This road has other large houses and is near the luxury hotels of the city. In fact this mansion, sometimes called the Ampang Palace, is the very same place where he stayed as a youth when he went to school in Kuala Lumpur. He bought it early in 1986 for Malaysian $15 million (about £4 million). The house was built post-war with Islamic motifs, topped with eight gold-coloured onion domes. It has two lounges, a banquet hall for 400, eight bedrooms and a swimming pool. As with his other homes, the Sultan has extensively renovated the property.

These properties are only those which have been discovered. There is little doubt that there are many others. But the list of properties which are known about is long enough. In summary, there is the biggest palace in the world, the Istana Nurul Iman; another palace, the Istana Nurulizza; other miscellaneous properties in Brunei, including several older palaces, some villas and extensive commercial property; the Dorchester Hotel in London; the Aviary stately home; 20 Kensington Palace Gardens, near the residence of the Prince of Wales; a house in Reddington Road, Hampstead; other houses in Hampstead Garden Suburb; another house in St John's Wood; the Beverly Hills Hotel, the Pink Palace; three other properties in Beverly Hills, one of which is to be made into another mini-palace; the Hyatt Hotel in Singapore and the Ampang Palace in Kuala Lumpur. Using the cupboard space in the Aviary and 20 Kensington Palace as a guide, he and his wives probably have a total of over 450 feet of cupboard space. These palaces, hotels and homes provide the Sultan with at least eleven different places in the world where he has rooms reserved continuously and exclusively for his own personal use. The richest man in the world may not be able to sleep in two beds at a time, but he gets as near to it as is humanly possible.

CHAPTER THIRTEEN

A Devil of a State

————— · —————

You become rich and your lazy Chosen People watch the coconuts
fall . . .

Anthony Burgess, *A Devil of a State*

The Sultan spends a lot of time in London, California and elsewhere
in the world, but in the end he must always return to Brunei. The
money comes from Brunei and so does his status, so he must return
and fulfil his role as Sultan. The duty of ruling his country is made
more bearable by the luxury with which he surrounds himself.
Anyway, the business of keeping control is not too difficult for the
time being. The people of his country are not rebellious. They had
the rebellion scared out of them in 1962 by the British Gurkhas.

Most of the well-educated Malay Bruneians have no reason to
rebel. They are very well off and secure in government jobs. They
pay no tax, they each own two cars and they live in spacious villas
with servants. The spread of Brunei's wealth among the upper
classes at least is shown by the traffic jams of smart new cars. The
number of cars trebled in the decade to 1981. The children of the
elite arrive at school in chauffeur-driven limousines. They jump out
of the back and walk into school carrying their books in Gucci
briefcases.

The expatriates living in Brunei also have a very comfortable
time. The businessmen and diplomats live in their large company
houses, they play bridge, they swim, they play a round of golf, they
play more bridge, they go to dinner parties and cocktail parties and
they play yet more bridge. One wife of a diplomat said she would

sometimes go to bridge parties seven days a week, and she would attend two bridge parties on some of those days. Meanwhile a humble university administrator said that during one two-week period he had been out to dinner parties on thirteen nights.

The lack of cinemas and other entertainments means that people living in Brunei are thrown back onto their own resources. This is the same sort of challenge, though much less great, that faced the colonial planters before the war, as described in the novels of Somerset Maugham. In fact, conditions faced by the employees of Shell before the war in Brunei were probably even more difficult than those Maugham's heroes experienced. Between 1930 and 1933, Shell employees were living in huts rather than wooden homes. A history of the discovery and development of the Seria oilfield states that in 1938, 'conditions in Seria at the time were grim'. Life there was 'rather dissipated' and 'spartan'. The author comments that 'most were induced to stay'. Presumably the rest took one look and left.

There were few roads, the jungle was impenetrable except by river and the rivers were infested by crocodiles. As late as 1959 there was a crocodile scare when a number of pet dogs were eaten and a housewife was scared by a crocodile climbing in to a drain behind her house. Shell tried shooting them, but was eventually reduced to hiring a local crocodile catcher who claimed to have disposed of over 700 crocodiles in his time. The biggest one he ever caught was more than twenty-seven feet long and was said to have killed twelve tribesmen.

Life in Brunei is safer now (except for the odd water-buffalo strolling across the road in the middle of the night), but the ex-patriates still have to make up for the lack of entertainment by being very socially active. Not, however, as socially active as they used to be. One long-timer still in Brunei recalls the 1960s, when employees of Shell, who are encamped together at the far western side of the country, would entertain themselves with the 'key game': the women would go to the bedrooms and the keys of the bedroom doors would be picked up by the men, as in a lottery. In those days expats judged the quality of a party by how terrible they felt the next day. But the 1980s has brought greater sobriety and propriety.

It has also brought 'young fogeyism' in the full form of the present British High Commissioner, Roger Westbrook. An ardent royalist, he willingly recalls the time on a previous posting that he translated for Queen Elizabeth.

The attitude of expatriates to the Sultan is shown by the words they use to refer to him. The hostile or neutral refer to him as 'the Sultan', the insiders who work directly for him show their status by calling him 'the boss' and the respectful call him 'His Majesty'. Westbrook refers, of course, to 'His Majesty'.

The expatriates also have their own words for the Sultan's two wives. They are called simply 'Number One' and 'Number Two', as if they were ship's officers. The phrases are used partly as a kind of code, to disguise the fact they are referring to the two Queens since in doing so they may well be showing what loyal Bruneians might consider to be disrespect. The expatriates love to gossip about the royal family and do so at great length. Royal gossip is the best game in an otherwise dull town.

Apart from the boredom, all seems to be well for expatriates in Brunei, and certainly many of them find it a lovely, relaxing place in which to live. But Brunei is not a tropical paradise. Many of the expatriates do not notice the fact, but there are poor and disadvantaged people in Brunei.

The average standard of living is high by Asian standards but there are many people a long way below the average. Just adjoining the capital is the water-village of Kampong Ayer. Wooden stilts hold the houses out of the water. The pavements are wooden planks and the lavatories are holes in the floor. Since the river is insufficiently full and fast-flowing, there is a visible build up of rubbish and human excrement.

The rich of Brunei and many expatriates knowingly say that one should look at the car park. And indeed there are a few BMWs among the older cars. The received wisdom is that these people like to live in Kampong Ayer and refuse to leave. Therefore they must be happy. Certainly one might prefer to live in Kampong Ayer, if the alternative was Kampong Kianggeh. This is another village adjoining the capital, approached past an open market. One crosses a narrow wooden bridge above a stream and comes to a shantytown of unpainted wooden shacks. A fire burns among some ruined buildings. Thin stray cats run away, a few dogs wander around and a couple of goats stand tethered. The paths between the shacks become muddy in the rains, so some bricks have been pushed into the ground to make the footing more secure. Carrying a modern camera and wearing clean clothes one feels embarrassed at having made a show of relative wealth. But if one offers a hesitant smile and nod of the head, one soon finds the smiles are returned more warmly in Kampong Kianggeh than in Brunei's marble palaces and government offices. Someone will try to exchange a few words in broken English. Another may ask to be photographed and proffer an address to which a copy of the photograph might be sent. It is, in short, like many a poor Asian village. The only difference is that it is located within a quarter of a mile of the centre of the capital. And three miles beyond that is the biggest palace in the world.

Prominent among the poorer people in Brunei are the tribespeople. But there are also Malay Bruneians and Chinese Bruneians. The Chinese in Brunei are generally more wealthy than others: they are the businessmen of Brunei. But despite their higher average wealth they have little reason to be happy with their lot. They face growing discrimination against them by the Malay Bruneian majority.

Asked about discrimination against the Chinese in 1986, Major-General Ibnu, now the Deputy Minister of Defence, replied, 'What discrimination?' This is the stock response. So, what is the discrimination?

The Chinese have not been automatically made citizens of Brunei as the Malays have. It does not matter if a Chinese person in Brunei can trace his ancestry there back three generations. He or she is still not automatically a citizen. In order for a Chinese to become a Brunei citizen, he or she has to pass an exam. The Malays did not have to pass an exam, nor did members of the indigenous tribes. The Brunei government argues that the exam is reasonable as people who wish to live in Brunei must speak Malay; it is the national language. The argument appears of dubious sincerity since many of the tribespeople in Brunei cannot speak Malay either, yet they are not required to pass the exam.

There is also a question-mark hanging over the fairness of the exam itself. The standard of Malay language required is, according to some, unnecessarily high. There also appears to be a hidden test the candidates must pass in addition to their language ability. It seems they must show 'cultural understanding' of the Brunei Malays. It must be said that there are Chinese people who have succeeded in passing the test. But one can understand why they would be reluctant even to try.

The question of citizenship is very important. Not only does it confer the security of right of abode in Brunei, it also gives a number of privileges and benefits. Only citizens enjoy the Brunei welfare state. Only they receive free education, free health care and subsidized housing. In some cases it is not even enough for someone to be a citizen to get a benefit: in the case of one housing benefit, the applicant has to be both a citizen and racially Malay.

As for jobs, only citizens can be employed by the government, the biggest employer by far. The Chinese consequently resort to business, as they always have. But now they find that Malays are given preference in getting government contracts. Malay companies are also given preference by multinational companies who want to remain in favour with the government. The multinational companies also feel bound to employ a high and increasing percentage of Malay workers.

The outstanding example of this is Shell, which is the second biggest employer, after the government. Over the last few years Shell has actively pursued a policy of preferring Malays to Chinese. Considerations of operational efficiency and fairness between one person and another have been put aside in favour of the dominant consideration – appeasing the racial policies of the Brunei government. Chinese contractors, even those who do menial jobs like mowing the lawns, have been ousted. The company keeps copious records to demonstrate how it is bringing on the Malays. The same records show by implication how prospects for the Chinese in the company have been drastically reduced.

Even Chinese Bruneians who have been given training schemes in Europe now find their prospects suddenly dimmed. These trainees used to be given permanent jobs on their return to Brunei, but in

1986 this changed and they tended to be given three-year contracts instead.

With the cards so heavily stacked against them, the Chinese Bruneians have been emigrating in increasing numbers. In 1986, not only were Chinese without citizenship emigrating, those who had succeeded in gaining citizenship were as well. In 1987 it was expected that about 2,000 would apply for (and in most cases obtain) immigrant visas for Australia. About another 1,000 are thought to have applied to emigrate elsewhere. This total of 3,000 must be considered next to a total Chinese population in Brunei of only 40,000 to 45,000, of whom many lack the qualifications that would induce other countries to take them.

Deep down, the Malay Bruneians are, perhaps, frightened of the ability and application of the Chinese. They fear being taken over by the minority. To justify this, they have convinced themselves that the Chinese in Brunei have no rights and should expect nothing. They wrap themselves in a sense of racial and religious self-righteousness.

At the Islamic Propagation Centre, two of the staff were asked whether they encouraged the Chinese in Brunei to convert to Islam. The cloudy answer amounted to 'not much'. But one of the devout Muslims quickly passed on to what seemed like a favourite theme. He commented on how the Chinese thought only of business and, by implication, neglected more elevated spiritual matters. He likened the Chinese to chickens.

The spirituality of the Malays in Brunei, however, is not always particularly impressive. On the surface, Malay Bruneians are devout in their Islam.

The government boasts that it checks more carefully than many other Muslim countries that the meat it imports has been killed in the approved Muslim way. The government brings in cattle live from its huge Australian farm (which is bigger than Brunei itself) and the cattle are correctly slaughtered with their heads facing towards Mecca and a prayer being said as the blood pours out.

Television programmes like *Miami Vice* and *Airwolf* have the kissing scenes and some other displays of physical contact brusquely excised. Men and women are shown approaching each other, then suddenly and inexplicably moving away again; the viewer is left to guess what happened in between. One expatriate went to the trouble of timing an episode which must have had a great deal of kissing in it. The normal playing time of the episode of *Miami Vice* was fifty-four minutes, but the version shown in Brunei was down to only thirty-two minutes.

There are religious courts at which the faithful can be punished for undue familiarity with the opposite sex. Consequently, one does not see couples holding hands in the street, let alone kissing. The Islamic Propagation Centre is looking forward to the day when adultery will be punishable by stoning to death.

Many women wear a 'tudong', which covers the head and hair but not the face. Prostitution in Brunei is apparently hard to come by. Alcohol and even entertainment are restrained and becoming more so. There are no discothèques and the only bars are in the few hotels catering to foreigners. Even these are in danger of losing their liquor licences. The Sheraton-Utama could not even get permission to have a classical guitarist.

No doubt there are many Bruneians who live up to this kind of asceticism, but many others do not. Members of the royal family drink alcohol and visit casinos in London. At the royally owned Polo Club, alcohol was still freely served in 1986 and 1987. After a polo match in 1986, Major-General Ibnu was seen drinking a glass of beer: he partially hid it and told a visiting journalist not to write about it.

The Sultan is consistent, at least, in speaking out against religious extremism, which he resists while showing a great deal of respect to Islam otherwise. He is very well aware of what happened to the Shah of Iran and does not want the same to happen to him. So the official state attitude of rigorous observance of Islamic rules of life remains and even tends to harden. At the same time, the large numbers of those who flout these rules find secret ways to do so.

Just as the elite likes to drink, so does the rest of the country. They drink in private or covertly. There are certain places where you can quietly be served beer from a tea-cup.

As for adulterous sex and other entertainments, those too are sent underground rather than relinquished. The rich go on trips to

Singapore or the Philippines with partners to whom they are not married or to find prostitutes. For the less well-off, it is a short boat ride to Sabah, where a village of prostitutes on the border caters to the frustrated men of Brunei. The suppression of the more usual sexual practices also seems to have driven the country towards a less usual one. Brunei has a small community of transvestites. Meanwhile, the relative wealth of the people means that many people have video-cassette machines, which are an effective means of getting round the censor.

But the gap between Brunei's public puritanism and actual appetites does not mean that Brunei is understanding of others. In their efforts to show their devotion to Islam, Bruneian officials show an increasingly intolerant face. It is not only against the Chinese that they discriminate. The Anglican Christians in the capital have not been able to get a permit for an Anglican priest to live there. A priest used to visit from Malaysia to hold services, but in 1987 he was turned back at the border. Quite possibly the Sultan himself would be angry at this incident if he knew about it. But the Sultan is hard to reach and is often out of the country, and the government beneath him is extremely inefficient. The clearest symptom of this is the large number of people it employs. Some 47 per cent of the total labour force (more than 50 per cent of the Malay Bruneians) is in government. There is, in effect, one civil servant to look after each adult citizen in the population. This is surely a ratio unmatched by any other country in the world. The closest comparisons can probably be made with Communist countries.

The government pays the Malay Bruneians in the government so well that they could not easily get other employment that pays better. The structure of the economy is simple: Shell extracts the oil and gas, the royal family takes a large slice of the profit and the rest of the profit provides money to keep Malay Bruneians in government sinecures. The Chinese pick up what they can by keeping the shop.

People who have dealings with the government tell of unnecessary delays, useless expense and senseless posturing. The construction of new public buildings involves the same kind of rush as the Sultan's palaces. A ministry will declare that a building will be finished by a certain date, say two years in the future. It then takes the majority of that time to obtain the design, agree it and commission a contractor. The deadline for the building, though, remains the same. So the ministry has to finance large overtime payments to get it completed in time.

A new road from the airport to the capital was built in 1986–7 and named after the Sultan himself. He was the first to drive along the road at its official opening: it was already uneven.

The government has commissioned a so-called 'Master Plan' for the future. A team of mostly foreign analysts has been studying the country in order to suggest in detail how it could develop. But having been hired at great expense and having examined the country in considerable depth, there are some people close to the team who believe that the plan will make very little difference. It could well be ignored. The commissioning of the 'plan' gives a gloss of activity to a substance of inertia.

Meanwhile government officials seem to become more and more convinced of their own importance. Whereas the Sultan's father used to go out to dinner with expatriate businessmen, now even Permanent Secretaries of ministries can be 'too busy' for a business meeting.

As for education in Brunei, an indication of its quality is that the best students and most ambitious parents want their children to study overseas. Brunei does have its own university. One of the reasons for creating it was to keep Brunei students from going abroad. It was thought far better to keep them at home where the Special Branch of the police could keep an eye on them and where they could be inculcated with the notion of 'the three M's – the Malay Muslim Monarchy'. This propaganda, like the bloated bureaucracy, is again curiously reminiscent of a Communist state.

The corruption in Brunei is similarly reminiscent. Its origin lies in the region where Brunei is situated. Bribes, backhanders and favours for 'cronies' are commonplace in business and government life in South East Asia. The 'cronies' in Brunei are those who are given certain advantages because of their connection with the Sultan or some other member of the royal family. Local companies with a member of the royal family or someone influential at court on the board have a better chance of getting contracts. Foreign companies are almost compelled to sell some shares to local interests and most of them pick a royal or royally connected investor. All this is under the respectable cloak of 'technology transfer' or 'teaching the Malay people business expertise'.

A member of the royal family wins two ways – getting shares below market value and perhaps also receiving a salary for being a director of the company. The amount of 'technology transfer' is derisory in most of these 'joint ventures'. Generally there is more technology transfer through employment of Brunei people which has nothing whatever to do with the shareholding structure.

One of the Brunei companies that has stakes in foreign companies is Jasra. This is Prince Jefri's company. The latest document it has filed (as at April 1986) at Brunei's Companies House consists of accounts to 31 October 1979. Despite its desultory attitude to filing accounts and despite the loss it made in 1979, which almost wiped out its small capital, the company succeeded in acquiring stakes in oil exploration in cooperation with Jackson, a Dallas company, and another stake in the local operation of Harrisons and Crosfield (one of the biggest of the traditional Far Eastern trading companies).

The lion's share of joint ventures has been taken by another company called QAF Holdings. This royal company has had, according to the records in the Companies House in Brunei, stakes in the following companies among others: Brunei Oxygen (manufacture and sale of industrial gases), Q-Carrier (sale and maintenance of air-conditioning), QAF-Solus (Offshore) (supporting services for offshore rigs), QAF-Reading and Bates (offshore drilling contractor), QAF Jack Tighe (offshore contractor), Dairy Farm (Brunei) (catering services), Fitzpatrick's (Brunei) (food wholesaler and retailer), The Island Development Bank (banking, since sold) and Boustead (auto and consumer goods dealer). QAF has also been involved in construction, so it has been in just about every business that matters in Brunei. QAF's 'partners' in these businesses are leading multinationals like Carrier and British Oxygen. In most cases the stake taken by QAF has been 50 per cent.

The biggest shareholder in this privileged company for most of 1984 was Parkwood Investments, at 301 Queens House, Don Road, St Helier, Jersey. In late 1984 Q A F, in a new corporate incarnation, got a listing on the Singapore stock exchange. In the process it had to reveal that by then its majority owner was Parkwood (not Parkwood Investments, but also a Jersey company) which in turn was owned by Princess Zariah, aged thirty-two, the wife of Prince Mohamed. Incidentally it was also stated in the same document that Parkwood owned 'several residential properties in the United Kingdom'. Alongside Princess Zariah on the board of Parkwood was Prince Ja'afar, who was listed as the managing director of Q A F as well as a director of ten other companies, most of which are in Brunei. This young businessman, then thirty-three, is the brother of Princess Zariah and of Raja Isteri. That makes him a cousin of the Sultan and his brother-in-law.

Q A F has done very well for itself in Brunei, getting large stakes in profitable companies run by foreigners. But when it ventured into Singapore and started buying businesses there, it lost money. Its strength was the royal connection. It could not manage so well when shorn of the advantage of cronyism.

Less subtle an abuse than cronyism is outright corruption. The government is, of course, against corruption. There is a special government organization called the Anti-Corruption Agency. But the corruption is so pervasive that the government felt it necessary to show an advertisement on television assuring people that the anti-corruption agents themselves were not corrupt. Extortionists posing as anti-corruption agents had been visiting shopkeepers demanding money for not prosecuting them.

The shopkeepers, though, are small fry. The big money in Brunei is in such things as taking bribes for making an introduction to the Sultan. Other corruption is the same as elsewhere in the region. It consists of such things as government officials ordering new buildings and taking backhanders from the contractor, or loan officers at banks granting loans to people who pay them bribes.

Brunei can legitimately claim that it once made a serious attempt to clean up its corruption. In 1982–4, Ponniah Rajaratnam was head of the Anti-Corruption Agency and set about his task with energy and expertise. He was a retired top police officer, experienced at fighting corruption. He had been Singapore's deputy commissioner of police and then director of the country's Corrupt Practices Investigation Bureau. His qualifications could hardly be better, since Singapore is the one country in the region which has tackled corruption with the determination necessary to achieve success. Indian by race and Singaporean by nationality, he was credited with being 'pleasant and hardworking'. A former colleague told a newspaper that Rajaratnam 'set very high working standards and always wanted his subordinates to emulate his diligent work attitude'. It is very likely that Rajaratnam went to Brunei with the approval and encouragement of the Singapore Prime Minister Lee Kuan Yew.

But his work ran into difficulties. Some of the people he was investigating were so senior that they were in a better position to have the Sultan's ear than Rajaratnam himself. He complained to one of his colleagues that it was very difficult in Brunei because there was a lot of interference and no cooperation from officers and heads of department. He told one of his colleagues that most of the 'big people' in Brunei were corrupt. But soon his diligent efforts would come to a sudden end. On 22 July 1984, he drowned.

There were many people under Rajaratnam's scrutiny. There was even one man (delicately called 'Mr D' at the inquest, despite the fact that he was dead by that time), who had told a clerk in the Anti-Corruption Agency, 'That Indian man is a bit too much. He better watch out.'

One senior person whom Rajaratnam investigated was Selamat Munap, who had held several senior civil-service positions. The Anti-Corruption Agency was investigating how Selamat Munap came to have enough money to buy a big house. Selamat Munap's wife also had shares in two of the five companies which the agency was investigating. Selamat Munap objected to the investigations; he demanded to know who had informed the agency and he said he would prosecute one of Rajaratnam's men. He threatened to 'report' Rajaratnam to the Sultan. In July 1984, after talking to a colleague about Selamat Munap and having had an hour-long telephone call with him, Rajaratnam referred to Selamat Munap as a 'dirty man' and 'a real bastard'. He regretted that he had not tape-recorded the conversation. On 19 July he instructed a colleague to inform the then Permanent Secretary at the Home Affairs Ministry that Selamat Munap was afraid that his past corrupt activities might be discovered as a result of one of the investigations.

Rajaratnam at this time was clearly very worried and depressed.

The fact that Rajaratnam had been investigating Selamat Munap and the companies in which his wife had been a shareholder emerged at the inquest. The name of Selamat Munap was not used in the newspaper reports. He was referred to only as 'Mr A', because investigations were still pending. This is the first time that his real name has been put in print – though his identity as 'Mr A' was well known in Brunei and it was indirectly revealed in a Singapore newspaper report which mentioned one of his government posts.

The 'pending' investigations which prevented use of his real name never got to the bottom of Rajaratnam's death. This is hardly surprising, given that as long as two months after Rajaratnam's body was found, his case was still classified as that of a 'missing person'. The police officer at the inquest said that he had no list of suspects or of people who might have committed foul play. The judge returned an open verdict. He said there was no evidence of foul play. The investigating officer, when asked what he thought had led Rajaratnam to the sea, said that Rajaratnam was very depressed. This implied suicide. The judge in his verdict said that suicide could not be ruled out. But suicide by a man who had already survived so much in his life seems unlikely. Nor is his death likely to have been an accident. He was not swimming. His body was found almost fully clothed.

Despite the enemies Rajaratnam was known to have made, there were no suspects. It was always, as far as the Brunei police were concerned, merely a case of a 'missing person'.

This may seem sickening and callous. But it provides no contrast to a picture of Brunei painted more than a quarter of a century ago. The main difference is that the British no longer play a major part. In 1961, Anthony Burgess published a novel called *A Devil of a State*. Burgess portrays the country of 'Dunia' as lazy, capricious and corrupt. The British who help to run it are depicted as second-rate figures pathetically trying to hold on to their ideals and dignity in the face of Dunia's demoralizing hypocrisy and inefficiency. The book was banned in Brunei and remains banned to this day. It is an open secret that Dunia is Brunei.

A Devil of a State is a rendition of late-colonial tristesse on the part of the British and feckless Third World arrogance. In the 1980s, under the rule of Sultan Hassanal Bolkiah, Brunei is much changed. It has modern buildings, brand new airport facilities, a more educated populace and full independence. But it still is unattractive in its hypocrisy, its incompetence, its corruption and its intolerance. Is there, then, an opposition waiting in the wings to bring change? Yes, there is a weak and wounded opposition. But the changes it wants are in some ways for the worse. In May 1985, the Brunei National Democratic Party (BNDP) was officially registered. The government removed some of the BNDP's best potential for growth by announcing just before the party came into being that civil servants would not be allowed to join any political party. This halved the potential membership. The party had hoped (perhaps optimistically) for 4,000 members prior to the ban. But in April 1986 it only claimed around 1,000 members.

The policy of the BNDP was the introduction of democracy. The party cordially invited the Sultan to continue as constitutional monarch. A large colour picture of the Sultan in full military regalia decorated the third page of the party's brochure. But the BNDP wanted the Sultan to have vastly reduced powers. They wanted him to be a constitutional monarch, like the Queen of England. Other policies of the BNDP tended, unfortunately, to be trivial or unpleasant. Far from criticizing the government for discriminating against the Chinese, the BNDP criticized it for not discriminating enough.

The Sultan allowed the party to exist for a few years. Then, on 27 January 1988, he shut it down. He also imprisoned without trial two of the party's leaders, Haji Abdul Latif bin Hamid, the president, and Haji Abdul Latif bin Chuchu, the general-secretary. At first it was not clear what had happened to the two men. No government announcement was made and it was left to the opposition to tell the world during February that its leaders had been arrested. Only in late March did the government confirm that the two men had been 'detained'. The detentions were said to be under the Internal Security Act.

In addition to the Internal Security Act, the Sultan possesses extensive powers under the State of Emergency proclaimed at the time of the 1962 rebellion. A 'State of Emergency' has existed ever since that date and continues today, regardless of the complete lack of any kind of emergency. It is doubtful whether the government has even respected the constitutional terms under which a State of Emergency can be declared and continued. But in Brunei no one can challenge what is, in effect, a dictatorship.

The Sultan has certainly gone back on his word of 1984. He said then in his Proclamation of Independence, '. . . Brunei Darussalam is and with the blessing of Allah (to Whom be praise and Whose name be exalted) shall be for ever a sovereign, democratic and independent Malay Muslim Monarchy . . .' The 'democratic' part has been forgotten. The Sultan's true attitude to democracy was probably revealed in an interview at the same time in which he said about political parties, 'We have experienced that before, in 1962, but it doesn't work out. It comes to chaos.'

Some people in Brunei argue that everyone is happy there and that no one wants democracy. But this flies in the face of the only evidence available. In 1962 when there was an election of members to a legislative assembly, the party seeking a change to democracy won fifty-four out of fifty-five seats. Nobody expresses any dissatisfaction in public because it would be like criticizing Communism in the Soviet Union (before glasnost). The only newspaper, the *Borneo Bulletin*, never discusses the possibility of a constitutional monarchy. Indeed the royally owned publication is so keen to avoid anything political that most of its front-page stories come from the neighbouring Malaysian states of Sabah and Sarawak. Only foreign publications ever carry the truth about Brunei, and they only are allowed to do it once. The *Far Eastern Economic Review* once carried an article critical of the regime and was banned for a few years. Any publication which is critical is prevented from being sold in Brunei and its journalists are prevented from entering the country again. Thus there is effectively censorship even of the foreign press.

For journalists who do get in, the task of finding out what is going on is difficult. It takes time and persistence to see government officials, who then reveal very little. Foreign journalists visiting Brunei are castigated by ministers for their 'coffee-shop' journalism. They are told they should talk to the government to get their information rather than listening to 'gossip'. But when the journalists visit and ask to speak to members of government, they are told that the government needs time to prepare for the visit of a foreign journalist. How much time? Three months.

The overall picture of Brunei is not all pretty. Corruption is abundant. Cronyism is pervasive and gradually becoming more obvious. The Malay Bruneians are treated to excessive numbers of government jobs while the Chinese suffer from disadvantages in every sphere. Foreign companies can do business there but many feel obliged to grant a stake to a member of the royal family or a crony. Excellence, efficiency, democracy, liberty, fairness under law and a free press are all aspirations that crumble quickly when confronted with the prevailing forces of self-righteous prejudice, intolerance, hypocrisy, self-interest, dictatorship and corruption. Yes, Brunei is a relaxed place. The living, for most people, is easy. But it is no model state and the Sultan, by clear implication, falls well short of a model ruler.

CHAPTER FOURTEEN

Holy Man with Diamonds

———— ڡ ————

Illustrated Weekly of India: 'But surely you know the Sultan of Brunei?'

Shri Chandra Swamiji Maharaj: 'Of course I do. He is a very close friend of mine. Very close. Do you know he has U S$25 billion? Yet he, a Muslim, worships me!'

Illustrated Weekly of India, July 20–26 1986

The Sultan's massive investment in the material world and the pleasures that it offers have not stopped him taking an interest in spiritual matters too. The Sultan could not be accused of having too few spiritual beliefs: he could more easily be accused of having too many.

He is a Sunni Muslim, but he has many other beliefs as well. Some would regard these as a Far Eastern flavouring of his Muslim faith. Others might regard some of them as outside the realms of Islam entirely.

The Sultan sees several spiritual men in Malaysia called bomohs: Muslims who claim to have special powers, who use rituals to bless or curse people. They also are employed to cure people of illnesses. A non-believer might call them witch-doctors. They exist in Brunei as well as Malaysia but since Malaysia is a much bigger country than Brunei, the leading bomohs there tend to be more expert. The Sultan flies to Singapore and then drives into Malaysia to see them.

In giving credence to the powers of bomohs, the Sultan is unexceptional among Bruneians. Even Azahari, the leader of the uprising against the Sultan's father, was in the habit of consulting a bomoh. Since Nancy Reagan took the advice of an astrologist, why should not the Sultan have his bomohs? Bomohs and astrologists probably have a lot in common, although bomohs claim to have the power to influence events as well as predict them.

A well-educated Singaporean who knows Brunei saw for himself a ritual dance there which was organized by a bomoh who had been hired by a woman and her relations. They wanted the bomoh to curse the mistress of the woman's husband. The wife, her relations and the bomoh all danced around the house of the mistress to effect this curse. It worked. Within a week, the mistress became seriously ill.

Even the multinational group, Royal Dutch/Shell, has used an exorcist in Brunei. On one occasion in 1956 a Mr Khiu Fatt was employed to rid a house of a ghost covered in blood which visited a house where a man had been accidentally killed. Mr Fatt, otherwise a vegetable seller, wrote signs on the doors and gave charms to the occupants of the house and the ghost was successfully exorcized.

As well as being influenced by Malaysian bomohs, the Sultan has taken the advice of Indonesian spiritual men. Magic and spirits are a major part of Indonesian culture and that country has many experts in those fields. The visible signs of belief in Malaysian and Indonesian spiritual men include objects that are supposed to offer luck or protection. The Sultan has worn a piece of wood around his neck to ward off evil spirits. Other things recommended by the spiritual men include a band around the arm with verses from the Koran, also to offer protection. And valued as offering luck and safety are the so-called 'horn' of a cat and black natural pearls, which are rare.

The Sultan has also consulted Indian spiritual men. One of them was given the use of the Sultan's suite at the Goodwood Park Hotel. He insisted on cooking his own curried food in the luxurious suite, creating a pungent smell that permeated the whole floor, which contains the other premium rooms and suites of the hotel.

Another Indian spiritual man who turned out to have a great deal of influence with the Sultan was Shri Chandra Swamiji Maharaj, one of the most bizarre figures in the Sultan's story. Shri Chandra Swamiji Maharaj ('the Swami' for short) is an Indian guru or spiritual adviser who was unheard of until 1986 but who by that time had amassed an extensive list of wealthy and famous followers.

The Swami is a large man with a chubby face framed by a head of vigorous black hair and a beard. Reportedly born in 1949, his real name is Nemi Chand Gandhi, and he comes from the Indian province of Rajasthan.

He is a spiritual adviser in a country where spiritual advisers are very common. Spiritual advice is one of the great industries of India.

The Swami has famous followers. He claims to have been consulted by Richard Nixon, Elizabeth Taylor, Indian Prime Minister Rajiv Gandhi, former Philippines President Ferdinand Marcos, former Prime Minister of Australia Malcolm Fraser, President Mubarak of Egypt, King Hussein of Jordan, John McEnroe, various leading politicians and film stars in India and many others. Photographs of him have been published with all those mentioned, except President Mubarak and Malcolm Fraser. There is also a photograph of him with Ryan O'Neal. He even maintains that he helped Elizabeth Taylor to succeed in losing weight.

One of the ways in which he gained attention and credibility was by performing acts that appeared to show he had special powers. According to one report, he went to Washington in 1983 and impressed a lawyer there by a demonstration. He asked the lawyer to write down on a piece of paper a name, a telephone number and a secret wish, and then put the paper in his pocket. The Swami successfully guessed everything the lawyer had written down.

Demonstrations like that impressed those he met and he combines them with resounding affirmations of the importance of spiritual matters over material ones. The lawyer introduced him to Washington politicians. The Swami also came to know show-business Americans and impressed them too. In fact, he willingly meets and gains the confidence of people all over the world, including people from Africa and the Far East. But they all tend to have something in common: money. By some curious accident of fate, his followers often turn out to be extremely rich. The richest of all, of course, is the Sultan. The Swami himself lives in luxury. When in Paris in 1986 he stayed at the superb George V Hotel.

One journalist in India, however, was sceptical about the Swami. He sought to interview him but the Swami, knowing the journalist's attitude, would not accept his calls. So the journalist, Pritish Nandy of the *Illustrated Weekly of India*, resorted to a technique of some audacity to get the Swami to grant an interview and condemn himself out of his own mouth.

Nandy persuaded a journalist on another magazine, not known to be dubious about the Swami, to seek an interview. Nandy went along posing as his assistant. The two journalists allowed themselves to appear favourably impressed with the Swami and they recorded every word. The following is an extract from that interview:

> Question. But surely you know the Sultan of Brunei?
> Answer. Of course I do. He is a very close friend of mine. Very close. Do you know he has US$25 billion? Yet he, a Muslim, worships me! Why only he? Even his wife worships me! Ordinarily, royal Muslim ladies don't even talk to outsiders. But I advise them even on their private matters!
> Q. The Sultan relies on you spiritually?
> A. Entirely.
> Q. Would he take decisions based on your advice?
> A. I told you that he and I are on intimate terms.

The Swami claimed that he was only concerned with spiritual matters.

> A. I am taking the message of Hinduism to the world. To 153 nations where I have travelled.
> Q. Who foots your bills?
> A. There is a divine spirit that looks after us all. We 'sadhus' have no money.
> Q. The divine spirit pays for your tickets, hotel expenses, fancy get-togethers?
> A. I have admirers and devotees everywhere, who look after my few needs. What does a 'sadhu' need?
> Q. Your needs seem quite expensive. Look at that diamond-studded watch on your wrist. You live quite well it appears . . .
> A. It is all His mercy. I don't earn anything. Things just come to me like that.

The journalists asked about the Sultan and Brunei. To impress them with his influence, the Swami said:

A. Why don't you go to London and meet him? I'll organize an invitation for you. He'll send you the ticket and pay your hotel bills and look after you very well. Very, very well. [Smiles] He goes to London during the polo season. That's the best time.

Q. But why should he invite me, Swamiji? I am just a humble journalist; not a man of God.

A. He'll invite you because I will tell him. You have no idea how much he respects me, he listens to me. He will do whatever I tell him.

Q. You have spiritual mastery over him?

A. I am not anybody's master. We are on intimate terms. That's all. You want to meet him?

Q. We have tried but failed.

A. You will not fail after I tell him. I'll fix the entire thing for you in London. Don't worry about anything. Money. Pleasures. He'll look after your *every* need. Do you know what you can get when you are the guest of the King?

Further to convince the journalist of his power and influence, the Swami gave them photographs of himself with numerous famous people. Among them was a picture of the Swami sitting on a sofa with the Sultan (bearded) and a woman who looks like Queen Mariam.

The Swami calls himself a spiritual man and claims to be unconcerned with material matters. But the style in which he lives and the things he says and hints at suggest someone who is out for the main chance. Later developments supported this view, for the Swami did not remain merely a spiritual adviser. As well as advising the Sultan on spiritual matters, he became embroiled in the affairs of the Sultan's friends, fixers and wheeler-dealers. He became a friend of Adnan Khashoggi. He was also a friend of the man who attacked Khashoggi's position with the Sultan, the man who bought Harrods department store in London and the rest of the House of Fraser stores group, the Egyptian who became perhaps closer to the Sultan than any other foreigner: Mohamed Al-Fayed.

CHAPTER FIFTEEN

Battle of the Arabs

——————— ❧ ———————

The most precious thing to me is not the money. It is my health.

Mohamed Al-Fayed, 1987

The Sultan, with his wealth, could have gathered around him any advisers and helpers that he wanted. He could have hired presidents of international companies or senior public servants. He could have hired from anywhere in the world – from Brunei itself, or Switzerland or the United States. He has indeed employed people from all over the world, but a disproportionate number of those he has taken into his trust have come from around the Mediterranean. They are not career businessmen or public servants or career anythings. They are independent entrepreneurs living on their wits.

Mohamed Al-Fayed is a balding Egyptian in later middle age. There is no doubting his charm and even his charisma. He can be blunt and emphatic, he can be quietly polite and he can be smoothly persuasive. To the other advisers and fixers he is a rival. Occasionally such rivals subtly denigrate each other. Al-Fayed has been known to refer condescendingly to Bob Manoukian, also from near the Mediterranean – Armenia – as a 'boy'. Bob Manoukian, in return, has been known to claim that Al-Fayed worked *for* him. But these are gentle digs among rivals. Among the entrepreneurs from around the Mediterranean there is another man who is not merely a rival of Al-Fayed but an enemy.

Adnan Khashoggi helped Al-Fayed in the early days. Their budding business relationship become strained when Al-Fayed had an affair with Khashoggi's sister, Samira, without Khashoggi's approval. In due course, on 16 July 1954, Al-Fayed married Samira. But then he left Khashoggi's business, with disagreement between the two men as to what was owing between them. He also divorced Samira. For much of the time since then they have been hostile to each other.

The background of Al-Fayed is a matter of controversy and even legal action. It is agreed that he comes from Egypt. It is also agreed that Al-Fayed spent some time in Haiti. But what he did there and in what circumstances he left is in dispute. It is at least clear that he was dealing with senior people in Haiti. It appears that he does not travel on an Egyptian passport. In 1964, Al-Fayed met Mahdi Al-Tajir, the ambassador of the United Arab Emirates in London and an extremely rich man. Al-Tajir apparently got Al-Fayed a Dubai passport and some important introductions.

With his powerful contacts, Al-Fayed won a contract to represent Costain, the major construction group, and Costain/Taylor Woodrow joint venture in Dubai. Between 1968 and 1980, Costain received work as the main contractor on projects worth over £500 million. Al-Fayed was paid for his advice and contribution to negotiations. The amount is undisclosed but would have been a minor percentage of the value of the contracts.

Al-Fayed's forte was becoming clear: his great ability was to emerge from nowhere, make contacts, obtain introductions and then start fixing up deals for others richer than himself. From this point he was able to go on and fully represent these extremely wealthy employers. In 1975, for example, he owned 20 per cent of Costain, but only as nominee for someone else. Among the extremely wealthy people he is claimed to have assisted are members of the Maktoum families. Al-Fayed is said to have a company which manages properties owned by the Maktoum families.

Al-Fayed was endowed with the most extraordinarily plausible manner. He seemed able to climb socially like a monkey up a tree. He understood that wealth could lead to association with prestigious people – through such things as sponsorship of events which the great and good attend. The prestige gained through such associations could be useful in commercial dealings. Thus wealth could lead to prestige, which could lead to more wealth. It was a virtuous circle. In Britain, he was invited to a dinner given by Mrs Thatcher for President Hosni Mubarak of Egypt. In July 1986 he was photographed in the company of Prince Charles. (He realized the special importance of polo and began sponsorship of a polo trophy at Smith's Lawn, a polo park owned by Queen Elizabeth.) In France, Al-Fayed was photographed with French Prime Minister Jacques Chirac, who gave Al-Fayed the Légion d'honneur. According to Pierre Salinger, the former press secretary to President Kennedy and recently ABC bureau chief in Paris, Al-Fayed was 'very close' to Chirac and had a 'very good profile' in France. He was appreciated for, among other things, restoring the Ritz Hotel to its former beauty, contributing money to the Pompidou Foundation (a charitable foundation of which Chirac is an important member) and for launching (initially with the Sultan's money and subsequently with that of the Ritz) the Ritz-Hemingway literary prize.

If Al-Fayed could succeed in getting so close to such people, it is hardly surprising that the Sultan was persuaded to put his trust in him too. When the Sultan turned to Al-Fayed, however, Khashoggi did not celebrate: Al-Fayed supplanted Khashoggi as one of the Sultan's top advisers and fixers. Khashoggi found that Al-Fayed, having previously argued with him and broken up with his sister, was now taking away his business too. When Al-Fayed got to know the Sultan, he counselled the young man that some of his expenditure had been too lavish, too ostentatious. In particular, he opposed the possible purchase by the Sultan of Khashoggi's yacht, the *Nabila*. Al-Fayed convinced the Sultan that Khashoggi was asking too much money for it – and he may have been right. Khashoggi was asking some US$90 million and, as we have already seen, the yacht was eventually sold in 1988 for less than a third of that sum.

By helping to dissuade the Sultan from buying the *Nabila*, Al-Fayed killed two birds with one stone. He denied business and profit to his old rival Khashoggi. And he appeared to the Sultan to be looking after the Sultan's best interests without seeking profit for himself.

Another item of expenditure that Al-Fayed successfully opposed was the acquisition of a Boeing 747. This 747 was ordered from

Carl Hirschmann, a Swiss contractor who manages, refurbishes and personalizes aeroplanes. Hirschmann was well connected. Enrique Zoble had eased his original introduction to the Sultan. Among the planes he looked after was the Boeing 727 Khashoggi supplied to the Sultan. The Sultan had also bought a Boeing 727 from Hirschmann 'off the ramp' at a Paris air show in the early 1980s. But this was not an altogether happy purchase as when he took delivery, the quality of the fittings was not of the absolutely highest quality. They may have been good value, but they were not the top materials that the Sultan desired and in due course he disposed of it. Either the Hirschmann 727 or the Manoukian one was given to Jordan. One problem with the 727s in general was that they could not fly non-stop to London. What plane could? A special Boeing 747, said Carl Hirschmann when discussing the matter with the Sultan. The Sultan said he would think it over, but no commitment was made and Hirschmann forgot about it. Then one day, a few weeks later, he received a banker's draft for over $100 million. No instructions came with the money to indicate what the money was for or even whom it was from. Hirschmann had to sit down and try to work out who could have sent it to him. He guessed it was the Sultan and then he was able to confirm that the Sultan did indeed want him to go ahead with customizing a jumbo jet.

The aeroplane was intended for the transportation of the Sultan, with friends, family and an entire string of polo ponies from Brunei to London without stopping. Work on the contract was started but then Al-Fayed persuaded the Sultan not only to cancel the contract but to give him a personal power of attorney to kill it. According to one source, Carl Hirschmann's son was in Brunei and was pressured by Al-Fayed to authorize return of the US$100 million. This he did – to the considerable anger of his father. (Indeed, father and son fell out so badly that the son left for America.) The part-converted plane, for the time being, sat on the tarmac at Basle airport while a dispute began over what compensation Hirschmann might receive.

Hirschmann felt that the dispute might benefit from the assistance of a mediator. A man was called in who was an old friend of Hirschmann and also probably knew and was friendly with Al-Fayed. He was Dr Ashraf Marwan.

Dr Ashraf Marwan is a softly spoken man who lives in London and works in a little Egyptian enclave of offices in Piccadilly, not far from Fortnum and Mason. He is married to the daughter of the late President Nasser of Egypt, a woman of considerable attractions and connections. Colonel Muammar Qadafi, President of Libya, was a great admirer of Nasser and remains a great admirer of his daughter. Indeed Dr and Mrs Marwan are among those few to have influence with Qadafi.

As fellow Egyptians and Muslims living in London, Marwan and Al-Fayed might have been well-placed to come to some sort of arrangement. But it did not work out. The two men could not agree terms and it may be that Al-Fayed did not like having one of his own countrymen opposing him. Thus the saga of the Boeing 747 reached stalemate for a while. Meanwhile, new developments and characters intervened which affected how the saga was eventually resolved.

In early 1985, Al-Fayed helped the Sultan buy the Dorchester Hotel. He entered negotiations with every appearance of doing it on his own behalf. The hotel was then owned by a consortium, including the company that managed the hotel, Regent International. Regent is part-owned and run by Americans, though its base is Hong Kong. The company began operations in the Far East where it grew fast. It then expanded back into the USA and also into Europe where the Dorchester became its flagship. Regent and the other members of the consortium received an offer from Al-Fayed that they could not resist, said to be various amounts up to £88 million. They sold out ownership to Al-Fayed, though Regent retained its management contract.

Regent was surprised to discover, within a few days, that in fact the new owner of the hotel was the Sultan of Brunei. Possibly it was always the agreed plan that Al-Fayed would front for the Sultan on the deal. But it is said that Al-Fayed bought the Dorchester for himself and intended to keep it for himself. He relented and sold it on to the Sultan, so this version goes, because the Sultan was so very keen to have the hotel for himself.

It has also been said that the Sultan particularly wanted the Dorchester and had done so for many years. But there is one other possibility. It is that Al-Fayed pulled off a particularly grand display of the fixer's art: getting hold of what the customer did not know he wanted until it was offered to him. If this happened, then Al-Fayed, knowing the Sultan liked the Dorchester, bought it and suggested that maybe the Sultan would like to buy. It might have been a bit of a gamble. If so, it certainly came off remarkably well.

It must be very likely that Al-Fayed made some money by passing on the Dorchester to the Sultan. But he was not finished yet. In addition to making money on the transfer of ownership, Al-Fayed was also hoping to make money out of the Dorchester in other ways. He wanted his hotel-management company to manage the hotel.

Al-Fayed was not new to the hotel business. He already owned and managed another prestigious hotel, the Ritz Hotel in Paris. He had refurbished it and was setting about using the charisma of its name to sell all sorts of other goods worldwide. This led him, in due course, into legal action against the cosmetics company Charles of the Ritz, challenging its right to use the word 'Ritz' in its name. Al-Fayed obtained a favourable result in a French court and consequently, as a lawyer involved commented, 'World War Three broke out'. Al-Fayed instituted legal proceedings all over the world, in about thirty jurisdictions.

These many cases have all slowly reached different stages. Most are not completed at the time of writing. But it appears that where proceedings have reached a final conclusion, Charles of the Ritz seems to be winning the day: so far it has won in Germany, South Africa, Indonesia and Canada. Being well aware of the commercial possibilities of using a famous name, perhaps Al-Fayed hoped to do the same with the Dorchester. Unfortunately for him, the tough American management at Regent International was not going to leave without a fight. They believed they still had the right to go on managing the hotel. Legal action began between the parties. Al-Fayed used not only British lawyers, in this case McKenna & Co., but also called in American lawyers, Williams and Connolly of Washington DC. The Al-Fayed side also hired international accountancy firms Price Waterhouse & Co. and Peat, Marwick, Mitchell & Co. They sent out a kind of 'hit squad' to investigate documents. These documents helped win the day for Al-Fayed. One person on the Al-Fayed side described the day of victory in 1986 as 'very thrilling'.

Under Al-Fayed's management, the Dorchester charged the Sultan, £1,068 per day (exclusive of Value Added Tax) for keeping his suite empty when he was not there. It may seem bizarre that the Sultan was charged at his own hotel at all, but the reason was probably that Al-Fayed's management company was paid a percentage of the profit and/or sales of the hotel and would have been unfairly handicapped if the Sultan had not paid a commercial rate.

Meanwhile, Al-Fayed was performing a much bigger coup. Al-Fayed was a friend of Roland 'Tiny' Rowland, the remarkable head of Lonrho, one of Britain's biggest international groups with interests worldwide but particularly in Africa and Britain. Some years previously, Al-Fayed had owned a stake in Lonrho and been a director on Rowland's board.

Rowland is a tall, formidable man with piercing eyes. His career has been a buccaneering one and he has often been in conflict with the establishment. Among the many highlights in his life was having certain aspects of Lonrho described by Edward Heath, the former Prime Minister, as 'the unacceptable face of capitalism'. He has certainly made some enemies in his career. On one occasion his private jet was examined by the customs service at Houston airport and he was found to be carrying with him a Russian AK 47 automatic rifle, a Thompson Commando Mark III rifle and a Python .357 magnum revolver.[1] Rowland, in resisting the difficulties these discoveries caused, told the customs official that he was a personal friend of Alexander Haig and his executive assistant Raymond Seiks at the State Department. Such high-level contacts are a normal part of Rowland's life. His contacts are particularly good in Africa, which is the cornerstone of his company.

Over the years, Rowland has bought and sold companies from all sorts of people including Daniel K. Ludwig, the reclusive American billionaire. In that case he was buying seven hotels located variously in Mexico, Bermuda, the Bahamas and San Francisco. Rowland

[1] *Sunday Times*, 4 August 1985.

also bought the *Observer* newspaper from another American, Robert Anderson, in Anderson's then capacity as chairman of Atlantic Richfield, the oil company. A friendly business relationship with him has continued since Anderson's departure from Atlantic Richfield.

In early 1985, Rowland found he had a problem. He had been working for many years to acquire the major stores group House of Fraser, the owner of probably the most celebrated store in the world, Harrods. His large-scale plan was to buy House of Fraser, move from that to buying the British Woolworth stores group and then continue on internationally to create a huge new stores empire. In addition, Rowland may have seen House of Fraser as a passport to prestige and to a better stock-market rating for Lonrho shares. He might also have been attracted by the latent property assets in House of Fraser.

But Rowland's attempts to buy House of Fraser had been frustrated at every turn. Lonrho had bought just under 30 per cent of the shares and made a takeover bid in 1981. The bid was referred to the Monopolies and Mergers Commission, which refused permission. Another time Rowland had tried to force the company to spin off Harrods as a separate company. This too had been thwarted. Then, in 1984, he tried to get people sympathetic to his own plans on to the House of Fraser board. For a second time, there was a referral to the Monopolies and Mergers Commission. The Commission took up the six months normally allotted and, to Rowland's frustration, got an extension to make further investigations. Then the chairman of the Commission asked Rowland why Lonrho did not sell its stake. Rowland took this as a hint that the Commission was going to thwart him once again. He feared that if permission for a takeover of House of Fraser was denied, the value of his block of shares in House of Fraser would fall. That was his problem and this was where Mohamed Al-Fayed came in. Al-Fayed was willing to buy Lonrho's block of shares.

From Rowland's point of view, Al-Fayed appeared to be an ideal buyer. He was sure that Al-Fayed was only just able to afford to buy the stake; therefore there was no danger that Al-Fayed would himself try to buy House of Fraser. Rowland could leave the stake with Al-Fayed knowing that, if the Commission decided to allow the Lonrho bid, he would probably be able to buy the stake back again, albeit at a slightly higher price. So Rowland parked the stake with Al-Fayed.

Then, to Rowland's astonishment, on 4 March 1985, Al-Fayed launched a bid for House of Fraser. Moreover, Al-Fayed's bid, unlike Lonrho's in 1981, was not referred to the Monopolies and Mergers Commission. Despite frantic opposition from Rowland, the bid very swiftly succeeded and, within ten days, the stores group which Rowland had worked and schemed for during seven long years was in the hands of Mohamed Al-Fayed and his two brothers.

From Al-Fayed's point of view, it was a brilliant coup. Al-Fayed had bought the near 30 per cent stake from Lonrho at a much lower price per share than he had to pay for the rest of the company: he had got the key stake in the company at a discount. Through having that key stake, he was able to get the rest of the company at a lower price than would otherwise have been possible. On top of that dealing coup, he had also won on the political front. Whereas Lonrho had been opposed every step of the way by the British Government and by the board of House of Fraser, Al-Fayed swept in with apparent ease.

His public relations, handled by Brian Basham of Broad Street Associates, was successful too. Articles appeared describing Al-Fayed as an Anglophile who came from a long-established, wealthy family. The *Sunday Telegraph* informed its readers on 3 March 1985 that Mohamed and his two brothers Ali and Salah were 'members of one of Egypt's most distinguished families'.

Rowland had thought that Al-Fayed was a safe parking space for the near 30 per cent stake. Al-Fayed had let him think so, then driven away with it. Rowland was extremely disappointed and angry. But he was not going to give up. He is nothing if not resilient and determined. First and foremost, he vigorously tried to persuade the British government to refer the House of Fraser take-over to the Monopolies Commission. One of his arguments was that Al-Fayed had used someone else's money to buy shares in House of Fraser. (The significance of this allegation was that if Al-Fayed had used someone else's money, then statements made in Al-Fayed's offer document would have been misleading.)

Rowland could not believe that Al-Fayed had possessed enough money of his own to buy House of Fraser. He had known Al-Fayed for many years and reckoned to have a good idea of what the Egyptian was worth. There was the Ritz in Paris, a castle in Scotland and some property in the USA. These and other assets all went to constitute a man who was certainly very wealthy, but not someone, he believed, with nearly £600 million in cash to spare. That sort of money, or some of it at least, he thought, had to come from somewhere or someone else. He had little doubt as to whom that someone was: he thought the man providing Al-Fayed with a financial boost was the Sultan of Brunei.

Rowland fed information and allegations about Al-Fayed and his relationship with the Sultan to various journalists. The information in all its defamatory variety was aimed at wresting House of Fraser from the grasp of Al-Fayed. Rowland was shaking the tree, hoping that House of Fraser would fall out into his lap. Most of what Rowland alleged could not be repeated because it was too libellous under British law. But Rowland could overcome this problem by having his allegations printed in the *Observer*, the newspaper which Lonrho itself owns.

Among the allegations which he published there (to the occasional embarrassment and anger of some members of the staff, who felt the newspaper's integrity was damaged) were quotations from what purported to be a very wide power of attorney allegedly issued by the Sultan to Al-Fayed. Also included in the *Observer* articles were remarkably detailed accounts of how money had allegedly been transferred from the Sultan to Al-Fayed and then on, by implication, to help pay for the purchase of House of Fraser. The purported power of attorney was signed prior to the House of Fraser deals and allegedly included the sentence: 'We hereby authorize you to operate on our behalf with Crédit Suisse, Zurich with immediate effect.'

Rowland claimed that three days after this power of attorney was signed, an Al-Fayed company called Hyde Park SA opened an account at a Swiss bank in Geneva called Compagnie de Gestion et de Banque Gonet. Into this account, said Rowland, were paid considerable sums, including US\$127 million from the Sultan's account at Crédit Suisse, Zurich. Rowland alleged that it was from the account in Geneva that Al-Fayed's takeover of House of Fraser was launched.

If all this were true, it would be strong circumstantial evidence that the Sultan either was the true owner of Harrods or else lent money to Al-Fayed to help the Egyptian buy it. Al-Fayed and his merchant bankers, Kleinwort Benson, asserted throughout that Al-Fayed had used nothing but his own money.

Rowland's campaign continued through the summer of 1985. Many readers probably became blasé about his revelations and stopped paying them any attention. One of the claims he made, was that Major Christopher Hanbury, of Southall, Middlesex, was on the board of Hyde Park S A. *Observer* readers would never have heard of Major Hanbury but, as we have already seen, he is the Sultan's aide in Britain with an office at the Aviary (hence his address being given as Southall). If he was on the board of Hyde Park S A and Hyde Park S A was a conduit for money which bought the House of Fraser, it followed, by implication, that the Sultan was involved in the purchase of House of Fraser. Another, admittedly wholly circumstantial link between the Sultan, House of Fraser and Al-Fayed which did not appear in the *Observer* was the fact that Al-Fayed gave Lord Fanshawe and his family a weekend at his hotel, the Ritz in Paris, to thank him for his assistance at the time of the House of Fraser deal. We have already seen that Lord Fanshawe has long been a friend of the Sultan.

But on the same day, 4 August 1985, as the *Observer* came out with its further batch of allegations, the Sultan himself emerged from his self-imposed silence. He issued a statement to the *Sunday Telegraph*. It said: 'His Majesty wishes to state . . . that neither His Majesty nor members of his family have, or have had, any financial interest in the House of Fraser plc or any of the Al-Fayeds' business.' This formal statement and the use of the phrase 'His Majesty', along with a picture of the Sultan in military attire with a row of medals, doubtless made the statement seem authoritative to many readers.

But some aspects of this statement were less than ideal. As with Rowland's allegations, the power of the Sultan's statement was weakened by its appearing in only one newspaper. Why, one might have wondered, had the Sultan not seen fit to make an open statement issued to all the newspapers? It was, at the least, a curious piece of public relations. Also the statement, although made in categoric terms, still left room for uncertainty as to the authority by which it had been issued. It was issued by an unnamed 'representative'. In other words, there was still room to wonder whether the Sultan would, at some later stage, be able to say that the statement was issued without his consent. Even so, the statement certainly was a body-blow to Rowland's campaign.

Rowland, though, was not deterred. He responded by releasing more details of the alleged transactions in Swiss bank accounts to the *Observer*, which also pointed out that there were discrepancies in the denials made by Al-Fayed and the Sultan. Al-Fayed's London lawyers had denied in a letter to the *Observer* the very existence of the power of attorney dated 24 August 1984. However the Sultan, in his apparent denial through the *Sunday Telegraph*, admitted the existence of 'a document dated August 24'. He called it an 'authorization' which had been 'given to solve a legal matter for His Majesty'.

After that, the battleground shifted with Rowland attacking the British Prime Minister, Mrs Margaret Thatcher, and her son Mark. The *Observer* gave voice to Rowland's allegations that there had been improper mutual assistance between Al-Fayed and the Sultan on the one hand and Mrs Thatcher and her son on the other. This allegation was one for which he was never able to offer much evidence. It was possible that Mrs Thatcher received jewellery from the Sultan on her very brief visit to Brunei in April 1985. But any valuable gift Mrs Thatcher might have been given would have been straightaway removed from the hands of the British Prime Minister and held by the state in accordance with well-established practice. Equally, though it is indeed possible that Mark Thatcher had visited Brunei and had been part of an attempt to obtain a construction contract there (something he has never denied), this is a long way from proving anything wrong with such conduct.

In 1986 Rowland reverted to a line of attack he had used from the moment Al-Fayed made his bid for House of Fraser. He cast doubt on the image which Al-Fayed portrayed of himself as a man of great wealth coming from a long-established Egyptian business family. The purpose of this challenge was to suggest that Al-Fayed had misled the former House of Fraser shareholders, the British press and the British government. If that was proved, then Al-Fayed would have bought House of Fraser on false pretences. A referral to the Monopolies Commission or else an inquiry set up by the Department of Trade and Industry might be forthcoming.

The official offer document by which the Al-Fayed brothers bid for House of Fraser referred to them as coming from an 'old established Egyptian family' with 'interests in the USA, Europe and the Middle East which include, in particular, shipping, construction, oil, banking and property'. A more detailed listing of assets and interests followed mentioning the Ritz Hotel in Paris, Rockefeller Center in New York and shipping companies based in Genoa, Piraeus, London, Dubai and Egypt.

The impression could be gleaned from this of large and varied assets built up over generations – all of a scale commensurate with buying House of Fraser for nearly £600 million. But the doubts which Rowland volubly expressed led the *Financial Times* of London to attempt to find out of what these assets really consisted. The newspaper's conclusion in a feature on 31 May 1985 was: '. . . extensive investigations have failed to uncover assets with a combined value of anything remotely comparable to the £615 million bid for House of Fraser.' 'A principal agency for Al-Fayed shipping interests', according to the *Financial Times*, was one of the Al-Fayed shipping companies called General Navigation and Commerce Company. This company was found to have a net worth in 1983 of £149,801 and incurred net losses in 1979–83 of £220,130. It was agent for an Al-Fayed shipping company in Genoa, Italy. This company was called Gilnavi SpA. It 'appears to operate just two vessels owned by the Al-Fayeds – a third was wrecked in 1982', said the *Financial Times*. And so the list of assets went on. None of them were in the same league as House of Fraser.

A year later, another journalist tried to discover the traces of the 'old established Egyptian family'. His article was published in Lonrho's *Observer*, although the journalist himself was a freelance writer. He went back to the places where the fortune of Al-Fayed and his family was supposedly started. What he found were traces of a family which was as established as any but not remarkable for established wealth. Al-Fayed's family, he wrote, had lived in a poor part of Alexandria. A resident there told him that Al-Fayed's father had been a teacher.

In putting the heat on Al-Fayed, Rowland had some assistance. Rowland already knew Khashoggi well, but now they both had reason to oppose Al-Fayed – Rowland because Al-Fayed had taken House of Fraser out of his grasp and Khashoggi because of their ancient feuds and their rivalry for the trust of the Sultan. It became apparent that some of the information that Lonrho passed on to the *Observer* and to other journalists came from Khashoggi. A Lonrho director once quoted to a journalist what the Sultan thought about Al-Fayed and the House of Fraser coup. When pressed on where he got such information he mentioned Khashoggi. Further enquiry revealed that some of this information passed through another hand, that of Dr Ashraf Marwan, the Egyptian trying to represent Carl Hirschmann in the long-running saga of the Boeing 747. Marwan clearly found himself in conflict with Al-Fayed, a conflict that was intensified when Al-Fayed sued him for libel in late 1984.

Al-Fayed was building up quite a team of opponents. Rowland, Khashoggi and Marwan make quite a formidable trio. The connections of each of them are tremendous; together they have access to information and influence in more places than some national governments. But it seems that another of the Sultan's advisers and helpers, Enrique Zobel, also joined forces with them. His addition to the strength of their loose alliance also presents an opportunity to describe the unexpected denouement of the Boeing 747 story, because he played a part in it.

We left the dispute when compensation for cancellation of the order was being handled by Al-Fayed on behalf of the Sultan, with Dr Ashraf Marwan acting as mediator. But then the power of attorney which Al-Fayed had from the Sultan was terminated (for reasons unknown). Enrique Zobel stepped in and obtained a mandate from the Sultan to end the matter. Zobel came over to London and there he met up with Rowland. It appears that Zobel, like Khashoggi and Marwan, was feeding Rowland information concerning Al-Fayed. It seems that there was no love lost between Zobel and Al-Fayed in their rivalry for the favour of the Sultan.

Rowland joined Zobel in flying to Switzerland to see Carl Hirschmann. Zobel's position was that Hirschmann should be paid little or nothing. Hirschmann's intention, in that case, was to proceed with legal action. Rowland, according to himself, persuaded the two men to agree on compensation of US$10 million. And that, it appears, is how the Boeing 747 saga was finally completed. The irony of the matter was that Rowland, the man who had opposed the Sultan's representative Al-Fayed, in this case actually helped the Sultan to settle a difficulty.

More bizarre still, though, is the possibility that this was part of an attempt by Rowland to get on friendly terms with the Sultan himself. Rowland's overriding ambition, it must be remembered, was to get hold of House of Fraser. Since he believed, rightly or wrongly, that the Sultan had helped finance the purchase of House of Fraser by Al-Fayed, who better than the Sultan to help him extract House of Fraser from Al-Fayed's grasp? To have pursued such a line of logic would have been typical of Rowland's radical approach. If he tried to get the Sultan on his side, however, it did not work.

In 1986, there were further developments on the House of Fraser front. Accounts made available that year showed that, as at 30 April 1985, the off-the-shelf company through which the Al-Fayed brothers bought House of Fraser had debts of £466 million. In other words, despite the assurances made at the time of the takeover bid that the Al-Fayeds were using spare cash to buy House of Fraser, they had, within a very short space of time, borrowed an amount that would finance the majority of the cost. This does not necessarily mean that they had been lying, since they might have borrowed the £466 million in order to free the original spare cash for other purposes. But the heavy borrowing would certainly have been consistent with the allegation by Rowland that the Al-Fayeds had obtained money temporarily from the Sultan, which they had then fully or partially repaid.

Meanwhile, the accounts of House of Fraser itself revealed that after the Al-Fayeds took it over, the dividend payout was drastically increased. The dividend for the sixty-six weeks up to 3 May 1986 was £19.2 million, compared with only £9.2 million for the year before. It became clear that the Al-Fayeds were using the dividends from House of Fraser to pay the interest charges on the huge loan in the Al-Fayed company. In other words, to a large extent the Al-Fayeds were using the profits of House of Fraser to finance the borrowing they had raised to re-finance the cost of buying the company. House of Fraser was, up to a point, paying for itself. But one consequence of the big dividend was that the House of Fraser group itself was becoming more heavily indebted than it used to be.

Al-Fayed, for his part, defended his reputation not by giving full explanations but by calling for his lawyer. He threatened legal action or started it against several journalists (including the author) and publications including the *Financial Times*, the *Far Eastern Economic Review* and, of course, the *Observer*.

Particularly interesting was the case of the *Financial Times*. He implicitly threatened to sue the newspaper for libel after it published its detailed analysis of his assets. The *Financial Times* settled the matter by publishing a statement alongside a story that quoted Al-Fayed's merchant bank, Kleinwort Benson, affirming, 'The Al-Fayed's acquired the House of Fraser with their own cash resources.' In its statement, the *Financial Times* conceded the falsity of one assertion in its earlier feature. The *Financial Times* agreed it was not true to say 'no one' believed the Al-Fayeds had bought House of Fraser with their own money. There were people, admitted the *Financial Times*, including the merchant bankers Kleinwort Benson and the Department of Trade and Industry, who had actually stated they believed as much.

This probably seemed like a humbling withdrawal to some readers. But it could equally be regarded as the writer being caught out making an overstatement which, in any case, is a manner of speech not to be taken literally. But anyway, the far more significant aspect of the *Financial Times* statement was the dog that did not bark. The statement did *not* withdraw a single word of all the material about the relatively small size of Al-Fayed's assets in relation to the House of Fraser bid. It is this assertion that still puts a big question mark over what really happened when Al-Fayed bought House of Fraser.

Nevertheless, the British government certainly seemed to accept Al-Fayed's bona fides. First, there was the fact that his bid for House of Fraser was not referred to the Monopolies Commission, despite the allegations of Rowland and the subsequent deeply researched article in the *Financial Times*. Second, there was the invitation to dinner at Number 10 Downing Street with Mrs Margaret Thatcher and President Mubarak of Egypt. Third, there was certainly a view in the British government that Al-Fayed, at worst, was preferable to Adnan Khashoggi as an adviser to the Sultan and, at best, was keen to do well by Britain. This latter view was that Al-Fayed wanted, as his prime ambition, to be accepted as part of the British Establishment. It was suggested that he had been trying to deliver to Britain the goodwill and help of the Sultan in order to gain greater acceptance. The idea that he might have some other ambition, like his own profit, did not have common currency in the British government.

If Al-Fayed had been able to deliver help from the Sultan to Britain, there is no doubt it would have been appreciated. At the height of the sterling crisis in 1985, the pound slid close to parity with the US dollar. The Sultan transferred US$2–3 billion into sterling to help prop up the British currency. By coincidence, or because Al-Fayed played a part in the transfer, the money was transferred to an account at the same merchant bank that Al-Fayed used to launch his bid for House of Fraser – Kleinwort Benson.

Meanwhile, Rowland continued his campaign over Al-Fayed's purchase of House of Fraser. The publicity which Rowland achieved for his allegations and the article in the *Financial Times* dammed up the earlier stream of articles about how Al-Fayed came from an old, established and respected family that started making its fortune in the nineteenth century. Al-Fayed, for a while at least, kept a low profile. There was even a lack of photographs of him. The same photograph appeared again and again in the articles about him. It was supplied by Lonrho, which got it from Charles Riachy, the Lebanese friend of Adnan Khashoggi and former manager of the Belfry Club. Riachy had taken the picture of Al-Fayed at a fancy-dress party. For he, too, knew Mohamed Al-Fayed. The connections in this world of Arabs and expatriate Arabs who served them were as complex as a bowl of spaghetti.

Rowland's continuing campaign focused increasingly on getting inspectors appointed by the Department of Trade and Industry to investigate the Al-Fayed purchase of House of Fraser. Rowland kept up a barrage of allegation and invective. He kept on seeking new information that would reinforce his case. He used his many and varied contacts and was willing to call on anyone, high or low, who might supply him with vital evidence. His forceful efforts were met with what he regarded as a major coup.

CHAPTER SIXTEEN

The Secret US$2-Million Tapes

———— ॐ ————

He has so many crooks around him and so many publicity and so many bad things.

Transcript made by Lonrho, allegedly of Mohamed Al-Fayed
speaking about the Sultan, June 1985

The person who supplied the information that so excited Rowland was the Swami. The Swami claimed to have made a secret tape-recording of a conversation between himself, his assistant Mamaji and Mohamed Al-Fayed. The tapes, so the Swami claimed, were made at 1 Carlos Place in Mayfair, London, on 6 and 7 June 1985, when controversy was raging about Al-Fayed's purchase of House of Fraser amidst the claims of Rowland that Al-Fayed had used the Sultan's money. Rowland flew to the Swami's headquarters in Toronto; he listened to the tapes. Having known Al-Fayed for many years, he was confident he recognized Al-Fayed's voice and that the tapes were genuine. He flew back to London and discussed the tapes with the board of Lonrho, which agreed that the company should pay US$2 million for them.

Accordingly, Rowland went with a London director of the Swiss bank, Crédit Suisse, to hand over a banker's draft for US$2 million to the Swami, who was staying with Adnan Khashoggi on the yacht *Nabila* (which Khashoggi still owned at that time). Khashoggi had teamed up with the Swami. Or perhaps it would be more accurate to say that the Swami had swapped sides. He had moved from friendship with Al-Fayed to friendship with Khashoggi. (One prominent person to whom the Swami and Khashoggi successfully offered their newly combined assistance, in late 1985, was President Mobuto of Zaire who, by coincidence, had lost his previous spiritual guide in a recent car accident. One observer commented that the Swami had come along at the right time for Khashoggi, to help him resolve his growing financial problems.)

Rowland later paid another US$3 million for other papers from the Swami. But these did not turn out to be as important as the tapes. Rowland had the tapes transcribed and issued to various people, including some journalists. Later he had the tapes transcribed again with the benefit of enhanced playback techniques to pick up some of the words that were otherwise impossible to make out. He sent out 2,500 copies of the transcripts, including several dozen copies to the Sultan, his family and other leading citizens of Brunei. He sent them to various bankers, brokers, solicitors and journalists in Brunei and Britain. He even sent a copy to every Member of Parliament.

Mohamed Al-Fayed denied the authenticity of the tapes. He said that he had not spoken the words attributed to him. This inevitably meant that either Rowland was issuing copies of a forgery or else Al-Fayed was lying. There was no middle course.

Bearing in mind that Al-Fayed has denied and continues to deny that the tapes are genuine, it is possible to repeat, within legal constraints, some of the conversations on them. If they do not show what Al-Fayed said in June 1985, they show what a forger wanted to put into his mouth. Despite Rowland's blanket mailing of the transcripts, excerpts from them have previously only been published in the *Observer*.

As in a genuine conversation, sentences are not completed and people reply to a point before it is fully made. The speakers continuously hop around from one subject to another. The Swami speaks in his own language, Hindi, which Mamaji loosely translates.

At the outset, Al-Fayed appears to have given something to the Swami because the Swami says in Hindi, 'The thing I need is your love, good feeling, mutual confidence – this I require. As I told you, these type of things are not required.'

Mamaji translates this way, 'Swamiji says I have desired some more valuable good from you. And the invaluable thing that you can give is your, love, affection, trust and confidence.'

The Swami continues to talk of love and affection and describes (through Mamaji) some of his philosophy. Al-Fayed appears to tire of this and wants to get on to other things, since he asks at one point, 'That's over?'

But the Swami continues, saying, 'My religion is humanity and its vestments are love and affections.'

A major theme of the conversations is Al-Fayed's opposition to other advisers of the Sultan, especially Major-General Ibnu and Enrique Zobel. Al-Fayed says that he does not want to hand over the Dorchester Hotel to the Sultan if the Sultan is going to pass it on to Zobel or Manoukian. Al-Fayed says he previously told the Sultan that if he wanted the Dorchester then it would have to be managed by the Ritz Hotel (the Ritz in Paris, which Al-Fayed owns).

Al-Fayed criticizes Zobel for encouraging media coverage of the main palace. He says you should not make a palace, then bring people from all over the world who make fun '. . . like *The King and I*, you see, in the film *King and I*. This is exactly the same story, and everyone was making fun of him, you know.'

Al-Fayed also bemoans the fact that Zobel, according to himself, has control of some of the security surrounding the Sultan. Al-Fayed comments that Zobel was 'out' for only three months before he was back. This probably means 'out of favour'.

But it seems that the Swami is by no means a simple ally of Al-Fayed listening passively to his condemnation of Zobel. The Swami says that he has talked to Zobel. He says Zobel told him that the Sultan had put a billion dollars at Al-Fayed's disposal. Al-Fayed replies this is rubbish. But the Swami continues, 'And his information is that on the basis of that, or by the support of that, you bought Harrods and made it an investment.'

Al-Fayed replies, 'But this is rumours, rumours, all rumours.'

The Swami reports that Zobel says the Sultan has received some of the money back and there is still some balance left 'which His Majesty has to recover'.

Al-Fayed replies that the Sultan would never tell Zobel this.

The Swami says, 'Major-General [this could be Major-General Ibnu, who is referred to earlier as a friend of Zobel] told Zobel.'

Al-Fayed appears to concede that such a line of communication is possible.

The Swami continues that Zobel says Al-Fayed is not returning the Dorchester to the Sultan. (This suggests that the Dorchester may still technically at that time have been in Al-Fayed's control, despite the publicized purchase by the Sultan.) Al-Fayed, presumably by way of reply, makes more criticisms of Zobel. He says the Sultan does not trust Zobel. He mentions some failings in the building of the main palace. He also claims to have saved the Sultan $400 million (what kind of dollars is not specified).

This conversation then becomes largely concerned with whom the Sultan trusts or should trust. Al-Fayed makes a point of saying how much he has helped the Sultan, especially politically. He says that he arranged for Prime Minister Margaret Thatcher to visit Brunei (she visited in 1985).

The Swami brings this line of conversation to a climax by saying that the Sultan had asked him whom he should trust more 'in the matter of money and advice'. The Swami reveals that he gave to the Sultan a kind of league table. Presumably to Al-Fayed's disappointment, the first name Swami gave was Zobel. Al-Fayed came next and the third was Manoukian.

But the Swami holds out the hope to Al-Fayed that he will use his influence with the Sultan to Al-Fayed's benefit. Al-Fayed refers to Major-General Ibnu, Pehin Isa (the Sultan's principal minister), Zobel and Manoukian. The Swami, through Mamaji, says, 'If I get your cooperation, heartiest cooperation, sincere – don't mind it then – you'll find that I'll have them all removed from the way.'

Al-Fayed appears to dislike Manoukian as much as Zobel. He calls him a 'terrible man' and offers the information that Manoukian got close to the Sultan through the Sultan's brother Prince Jefri. Elsewhere Al-Fayed remarks of Manoukian, 'He is Armenian, Armenian people worse than the Jews [laughter], worse than the Jews.'

Looking to his own claims to be the Sultan's trustworthy adviser, Al-Fayed makes the point that he does not pay off people close to the Sultan [one person is named]. He says, 'Because I don't need to pay [person named] to have things from the Sultan.'

Al-Fayed again makes some claims about how the Sultan trusts him. '. . . He [the Sultan] can't sleep at night without my people around, somehow because he trusts my people. He has my own butler, the butler who feeds me . . . dark, tall, he was the . . . Duke of Windsor's butler. He is with the Sultan all the time . . . He is the man in charge, makes breakfast for the Sultan . . .'

This is a reference to the late Duke of Windsor's black butler, Sidney, who has indeed acted as a butler for the Sultan. It is quite credible that Al-Fayed arranged this, since Al-Fayed obtained control of the late Duke of Windsor's villa near Paris after the death of the Duchess. The French government leased the villa to him for fifty years on condition that he restored it.

The Swami uses the conversation to find out what he can. He asks a number of questions, eliciting information from Al-Fayed about Zobel, Ibnu, Manoukian, Singapore Prime Minister Lee Kuan Yew, Queen Mariam and Saddique (a businessman based in Singapore who for a time was managing director of the royal company, QAF).

Meanwhile, mixed in with the criticisms, intrigue and probing are protestations of friendship, philanthropy and religion. Mamaji, presumably on behalf of the Swami, gives a guarantee to Al-Fayed of another thirty years of 'lively life'. Al-Fayed says how he wants to help the Sultan and wants the Sultan to help various good causes. Mamaji says, 'Let us join hands to help our common friend for his better achievement and success in life.' Al-Fayed says he has asked the Sultan to help Egypt and to help in Jordan. He mentions Afghanistan and says, 'A lot of people, orphan people have no homes, all this, I want him to help them.'

They all agree that the Sultan is a nice man. But Al-Fayed worries about the people around him saying, 'He is not a strong person you know. He is a kind person and it's difficult, you know, with those people, because they are bad people.' He also says, 'He has so many crooks around him and so many publicity and so many bad things.'

That, at least, is something with which most observers of the Sultan would agree.

Why, if the tapes were genuine, did the Swami make them? Did he guess that he might be able to sell them for US$2 million? Another answer is suggested by claims made by a Dr Prathap Reddy in *Forbes* magazine of 7 March 1988. Dr Reddy, described as a prominent physician and a follower of the Swami, claimed that in early 1985 he attended a meeting in the Royal Holiday Inn in Singapore at which the Sultan talked to the Swami. Dr Reddy is quoted as saying, 'The Sultan told Swamiji that he had given US$ 900 million to Mohamed Al-Fayed. But now the Sultan was uneasy about the whole thing. The Sultan asked Swamiji how he could get his money back.'

This claim is consistent with the claim made by Rowland that the tapes were played to the Sultan by the Swami very soon after they were recorded. The implication of these allegations is that the Swami made the tapes as part of his efforts to help the Sultan assess Al-Fayed. If genuine, the transcript reflects a way of life like that of a medieval court. The barons make whatever progress and profit they can for themselves while trying to prevent other barons supplanting them in the favour of the king. And all of them protest that they act for the love of king, country and mankind. The Swami appears a sort of Cardinal Wolsey figure, clearly as interested in the temporal world as the divine, despite his repeated statements about religion and spirituality.

But Al-Fayed maintains that the words ascribed to him were fabricated. Rowland, he implies, was peddling a forgery.

Others, too, did not pay the transcript much attention at all. According to Richard Hall in his book on Rowland, *My Life with Tiny*, even journalists at the *Observer* gave it short shrift. The first transcript lay around on the news-desk of the *Observer*, but 'nobody could extract much sense from it'.

This is easily understandable, since at that time few British journalists would have heard of Enrique Zobel, Bob Manoukian, Major-General Ibnu, Saddique or Pehin Isa. References in the transcripts to 'Geoffrey' would have meant nothing to them (though anyone who has read this far will immediately realize, when reading the transcript, that the reference is to Prince Jefri and that his name has been spelled in the English way by the transcriber). For most people in 1985, a reference to the death of a Singaporean investigator would have been utterly mysterious. Also adding to the confusion was the fact that the sequence of the conversations was incorrect in the first transcript and was only put right in the 1987 version.

At the time of writing, it has not been proved whether the tapes are forgeries or genuine.

A representative of the Swami reportedly gave Al-Fayed an affidavit stating that the Swami never made any recording implicating Al-Fayed. But an aide of the Swami reportedly told a Rowland ally that the Swami would sign an affidavit supporting whatever Rowland wanted if Rowland would help him out of a new difficulty he had encountered, of which more later.

What would a forger have needed to do to create the tapes? First, he would have had to find an actor who could sound like Al-Fayed. Next, he would have had to write a script. In writing this script he would have needed access to a great deal of information about the Sultan and many of his foreign advisers. He would also have needed to be informed about such local matters as the death of Rajaratnam. Such a variety of information – some from Europe or the United States and some from Brunei – might have been available to the Swami or Al-Fayed or perhaps certain members of the royal family – but not to many.

Then, in using this information, the forger would have had to make the curious and brave decision to use it. This would have been curious because most people in Britain, where it was to be used, would never have heard of all the people and events mentioned and would consequently be confused by it – as were the *Observer* journalists, who were better informed on these subjects than most. The forger would also have been brave, because of the risk that Al-Fayed would immediately offer himself for a voice test which would straightaway disprove the authenticity of the tapes and bring upon the forger the formidable wrath of Rowland, who paid US$2 million for them.

Finally, the forger would have made the eccentric decision to avoid putting into Al-Fayed's mouth the words which Rowland most wanted to hear. Rowland would have liked Al-Fayed to admit in the tapes that he had bought House of Fraser with the Sultan's money. But the forger makes Al-Fayed say nothing of the kind. The Al-Fayed of the tapes calls it all 'rumours'. It makes a less than completely satisfactory tape for Rowland. It makes our forger a bizarre sort of man.

In the end, the main importance of the tapes has turned out to be not so much the words in it as the fact that Al-Fayed denied that they were genuine. That made the tapes a test of the truthfulness of Rowland and Al-Fayed. If Al-Fayed turned out to be a liar, then how could one believe other statements he had made about the provenance of the money with which he bought the Harrods empire?

Al-Fayed himself, meanwhile, was busying himself with making changes at the stores group. He used House of Fraser to buy Turnbull and Asser, a shirt shop in posh Jermyn Street (the same street as Manoukian's Vincci clothes shops). Never reluctant to associate himself with prestige in general and royalty in particular, Al-Fayed probably bore in mind the fact that Prince Charles bought his shirts and ties at Turnbull and Asser.

Al-Fayed also embarked on a claimed £200 million re-furbishment programme for Harrods. Meanwhile, the managing director he inherited, Professor Smith, soon left. He was replaced by an Australian, Brian Walsh. But he left too, in 1987, to be replaced by Al-Fayed himself. Having had no experience of running retail operations before, Al-Fayed is now running one of the biggest stores groups in the world. The group was, however, becoming less big, since Al-Fayed gradually sold off stores to realize their property value. This caused ostensible outrage from Lonrho. But in fact it was a logical move, since many of the stores were not making a good return on capital. Lonrho might well have done the same if it had succeeded in buying House of Fraser itself.

While Al-Fayed sold stores, he bought shares. The shares he bought were in Sears, another major British stores group, which owns the giant Selfridges store dominating Oxford Street. Al-Fayed might have noticed that Sears also owned a very prestigious outlet in Regent Street: Garrard, the Crown Jewellers.

Al-Fayed even got close, for a short while, to Queen Elizabeth. In May 1987 he was with her at the Royal Windsor Horse Show, where Harrods sponsored the Harrods Driving Grand Prix. The Queen presented the prizes, with Al-Fayed in close attendance. Al-Fayed also obtained contact with the royal family through his undertaking to restore the late Duke of Windsor's home in Paris. The house, according to a source close to Al-Fayed, included one or more objects of interest to the royal family.

Al-Fayed also did not neglect to keep up and enhance his friendly relations with the Sultan. The bad publicity over House of Fraser did not appear to deter the Sultan from receiving Al-Fayed. The Egyptian visited Brunei several times during 1987. He also pursued a project rather like the book which Enrique Zobel had commissioned about the Sultan and Brunei. Al-Fayed wanted to go one better than a book, and so he commissioned a film.

While Al-Fayed was making his strategic business moves and maintaining his relationship with the Sultan, his enemy Rowland was still waging war on him. Numerous legal actions were in progress between them, though they seemed to be a long time actually getting into the court room. Each side made the most of the legal 'discovery' process, whereby each side may demand to see relevant papers owned by the other.

Charles Riachy tried to make peace between them. He knew Al-Fayed of old (hence the picture he had taken of Al-Fayed at the fancy-dress party) and he was friendly with Rowland. But Rowland refused to consider relenting.

Then Rowland at last had his day. One of the legal proceedings pursued by Lonrho was an attempt to compel the government to refer the House of Fraser takeover to the Monopolies and Merger Commission. The attempt failed, but the judge made it plain that further investigation of the matter was warranted. Shortly after that, in April 1987, came a government announcement of an inquiry into the circumstances of the takeover of House of Fraser by Al-Fayed. The activities of Lonrho would also come into the ambit of the inquiry, but clearly this was a victory for Rowland's persistence. Al-Fayed, having been welcomed into centre-stage of British business, was suddenly going to have to answer questions from government-appointed inspectors. He was quoted as saying, 'I am hurt. I have given a large part of myself to this country, which became my home. A government which I helped in ways of great importance has shown me no respect.' He added, in reference to Rowland, 'A dog barked and the ministers listened.'

Rowland had every reason to feel triumphant. But not for long. In October the same year his friend Adnan Khashoggi gave evidence to these inspectors. Khashoggi gave his evidence at the house of his friend Charles Riachy (which is in the Boltons, one of the most fashionable enclaves of Chelsea). Lawyers acting for Lonrho were present at the interview and reported back to Rowland that they thought the inspector, Henry Brooke QC, could be forming the view that Khashoggi's evidence was suspect. The lawyers also got the impression that the inspector was tending to believe the Al-Fayed version of the facts.

Thus alerted, Rowland returned to the offensive. He sent the inspectors a barrage of letters making demands and allegations, even including a suggestion that Brooke was compromised by being the brother of the recently appointed chairman of the Conservative Party. Lonrho produced a superior, printed version of the tapes, cheekily entitled, 'The Sultan and I, by Mohamed Al-Fayed'. Rowland then deputed another director of Lonrho, Robert Dunlop, to go on a worldwide research mission to amass documents and evidence that would compel the inspectors, so Rowland hoped, to accept that his version was the true one. Dunlop went on his mission while Rowland also persuaded other people who would support his case to give evidence to the inspectors. He even flew people over from Haiti to testify about Al-Fayed's time in that country.

The evidence collected by Dunlop was presented and more people gave evidence. By the end of February 1988 Rowland believed that his bombardment of the inspectors had borne fruit. He believed the inspectors were 'onside'. The pendulum, he thought, had swung back in his favour. But he continued to work to cement the victory he hoped for. He obtained a copy of an LBC Radio tape of Al-Fayed speaking. Unfortunately for Rowland, Al-Fayed did not say much on the tape. He was opening the 1988 Harrods' winter sale and only said, '5–4–3–2–1'. Rowland did better with a tape-recording supplied by Dr Marwan, who had taped some of his conversations with Al-Fayed.

One of Rowland's more ambitious aims was to obtain the testimony of the Sultan himself. He was willing and eager to offer the Sultan protection from such things as legal action. In theory, if the Sultan's money in fact had been used, Rowland might have had a legal case against the Sultan. The big firm of solicitors, Clifford Chance, represented the Sultan in England. But Rowland did not want to get the Sultan, he wanted to get Al-Fayed. The difficulty was that Rowland could not easily reach the Sultan to try to arrange a deal.

His efforts to reach the Sultan included asking President Kenneth Kaunda of Zambia (an old friend of Rowland) and Rajiv Gandhi, Prime Minister of India, to talk to the Sultan during the meeting of Commonwealth Heads of Government in Canada in October 1987. He sent the Sultan a letter on 30 November 1987, along with the enhanced copy of the transcript. He got no reply at all. So in February 1988 Rowland was still seeking to get his message across to the Sultan and still using contacts at the highest possible level. But he clearly was having no success by 25 March because on that date he issued, at Lonrho's heavily attended annual general meeting of shareholders, a glossy brochure that was unflattering to the Sultan. The front of the brochure was illustrated with a colour picture of the Sultan under which was the caption, 'A fool and his money . . .' The brochure contained a collection of facsimiles of documents, photographs and affidavits supporting Rowland's allegations about Al-Fayed and House of Fraser.

Shareholders at the same annual general meeting were also offered another document. As shareholders came to the doorway of the Grosvenor House Hotel in Park Lane, several attractive women and a few men handed out a document issued by Al-Fayed, questioning aspects of Lonrho's accounts. The previous year people acting for Al-Fayed had actually asked questions in the meeting but in 1988 the representative, despite being a barrister, kept quiet. The government-appointed inspectors completed their report and submitted it to Lord Young, the minister at the Department of Trade and Industry, on 23 July 1988. Much to Rowland's frustration, no doubt, the report was not published straightaway. But on 29 September, the Lonrho camp rejoiced at the news that Lord Young had passed the report to both the Serious Fraud Office and the Office of Fair Trading (which would consider recommending a reference to the Monopolies and Merger Commission). A government official was quoted as saying 'Serious issues have been raised by our report which are required to be looked at by the prosecuting authorities.' A Lonrho director said he felt 'as if we had won a race in the Olympics'. The Al-Fayed camp stoutly maintained it was 'not surprised ' in view of the pressure brought to bear by Lonrho.

Meanwhile Rowland's contacts in the government of India helped him keep in touch with what was happening to the man who had supplied him with the tapes. The Swami, having pocketed, as far as Rowland knew, the tidy sum of US$5 million for supplying the tapes and other documents, was arrested in India on charges of breaking India's foreign-exchange regulations. That was the 'difficulty' referred to earlier which the Swami had encountered. He was allowed out on bail, but his passport was confiscated and Rowland considered, with apparent satisfaction, that the Swami would not be allowed out of India during the whole of 1988. That was in February. In fact it was Rowland himself whose 'representations' had caused the arrest of the Swami.

Rowland's apparent dissatisfaction with the Swami seemed connected with attacks made on the authenticity of a document that the Swami had supplied in the US$5 million package. This document, dated 4 November 1985, stated that Mark Thatcher had visited Brunei from 24 to 26 October 1984 in the company of Al-Fayed. But since the authenticity of the document was under attack by Al-Fayed, Rowland wanted to track down Dato Haji Mohamed Ali bin Haji Mohamed Daud, who was the apparent signatory. His title, given on the document, was Permanent Secretary, Minister of Home Affairs. Rowland wanted to find Dato Mohamed Ali to see whether he would confirm that he had signed the document. One Lonrho director said it would be 'worth the while' of a journalist he was talking with to find this man. Rowland either wanted Dato Mohamed Ali to confirm he signed the document or else he wanted back the money he had paid for the document, if it was false. Meanwhile, until the issue was resolved, Rowland appeared content that the Swami should be in India – without a passport.

That was not the end of the Swami's problems, which were becoming extremely complicated and which again involved the Sultan. By a bizarre set of circumstances, the Sultan even found himself being mentioned in articles that were primarily concerned with a major arms scandal in India. The Swami had long been involved in Indian politics and had not made himself popular with all members of the Gandhi administration. As a result, he wanted information damaging to his enemies. He thought such information would protect him against them. This, it seems, was his reason for seeking interviews with Martin Ardbro, who was knowledgeable about a government bribery scandal. Martin Ardbro was the former president of the Swedish arms manufacturer, Bofors, which had won a contract to supply howitzers to India in March 1986. The contract had become a major scandal in India because of alleged kickbacks. The Swami interviewed Ardbro in Vienna and Paris in September 1987. The diaries of Ardbro have since confirmed this and also indicated that both Khashoggi and the Sultan were present at these meetings.

The alleged presence of the Sultan at these meetings was supposedly because he was ready to offer Ardbro the bait of a lucrative job. This bait was supposed to encourage Ardbro to tell the Swami all that he knew about the Bofors scandal. But the Sultan's participation in this business, if true, would be very curious, since it would indicate a somewhat reckless willingness to become involved in Indian politics, not to mention a surprising re-opening of his previously discontinued relationship with Khashoggi. As for the Swami, if his motive had indeed been to provide himself with information that would protect him from attack by the Indian government, it did not work. He was arrested immediately following his arrival in India, on 19 September 1987.

Then, in an even more extraordinary development, in early 1988 the Swami was alleged to be part of a plot to unseat Gandhi. This plot was alleged by the former President of India, Zail Singh, who alleged that the Swami had offered him Rupees 400 million (US$30.8 million) to pay for a campaign against Gandhi's nominee for the presidency. The idea was that Singh would be re-elected and then replace Gandhi with a senior cabinet minister, P. V. Narasimha Rao. This minister, implicitly, was preferred by the Swami. How was the Swami to obtain this US$30.8 million? Singh maintained that the Swami had told him he was close to many extremely rich people including, reportedly, 'an oil-rich sheik'.

That was the confused state of play in spring 1988. The Byzantine manoeuvrings of the Sultan's foreign advisers could not always be fully explained. But it was at least clear that these past and present advisers of the Sultan were not an altogether happy group of people. The Swami had been arrested in India and had his passport taken away. Adnan Khashoggi, notwithstanding his cooperation with the Swami, had come to grief in several ways. The toppling of President Marcos had hit him, since he had been developing large investments in the Philippines with Marcos at the time when Aquino took power. Khashoggi's relationship with the Marcoses was so close that he stored Impressionist and Post-Impressionist masterpieces for them. In fact, his penthouse suite in Cannes was raided in a search for the pictures by French police in May 1987. Then in October 1988, Khashoggi was indicted in New York on charges of helping Marcos conceal his ownership of various assets. Khashoggi had played a seminal part in the Iran–Contra affair and lost money on that score too. He had been forced to lose his beloved yacht *Nabila* and to sell several other major assets to shore up his finances. In America his company in Salt Lake City, called Triad, had been forced to file for protection under Chapter 11 of US bankruptcy law. Khashoggi had suffered a remarkable catalogue of misfortune.

Meanwhile his old enemy, Mohamed Al-Fayed, had, at least, successfully managed to buy the House of Fraser stores group. But his claims about his wealth had been prominently rebutted in the *Financial Times*. Worse still, the British government had appointed inspectors to investigate his purchase of House of Fraser and then passed the report to the Serious Fraud Office. Enrique Zobel was still in business, but he, too, had come down a peg. He had lost his top position in Philippines business by quarrelling with his family and, like Khashoggi, backing Marcos at the wrong time.

Bob Manoukian, alone among these advisers, was not known to have suffered some setback.

It was as if the gaining of advantage through knowing the Sultan had some sort of curse attached. Perhaps the Sultan's extreme wealth attracted people whose ambition was excessive to the extent of being dangerous even to themselves. Four out of five had met major difficulties. But there were six foreign advisers of the Sultan. What had happened to the sixth?

CHAPTER SEVENTEEN

Chicanery and Conspiracy

———————— ☙ ————————

However much one considers local and family conditions, dishonesty is the same whichever culture one is in.

Justice Barry Mortimer, summing up at the end of the National Bank of Brunei trial.

Brunei, February 1988

If there are themes in all the variety of things that happen to and around the Sultan, they are themes of chicanery, conspiracy, corruption, mystery and excess.

In 1986 and 1987 events took place in Brunei that certainly included some of these themes. One of them concerned the sixth foreign adviser of the Sultan – a very prominent businessman and one-time billionaire, Tan Sri Khoo Teck Puat. Racially Chinese, Khoo started his career in Singapore but later became a citizen of Malaysia. Then he went to Australia and became a permanent resident there. Now his whereabouts are a mystery, although there have been reports of him being seen in Taiwan, Thailand and Britain.

Unlike the other foreign advisers, Khoo is austere. He dresses in a dull suit and wears glasses with powerful lenses in old-fashioned frames. He looks more like an old tailor than a business maverick, but 'business maverick' is what he is. He works on a large scale with assets spread far and wide. He is ambitious and determined.

He first made his mark in Singapore, where he progressed quickly up the ladder of Overseas-Chinese Banking Corporation during the Second World War, when the Japanese were in occupation. His rise continued after the war until he was near the top of the bank. Then he realized that someone senior to him would block his rise to the chief-executive position. So in 1960 he went to neighbouring Malaysia and began a bank of his own. This bank, the Malayan Banking Corporation, grew very fast with the backing of the ruling Malay political party. But then Khoo again fell out with board members of the bank; he had invested a lot of the bank's money in Singapore and lent a considerable amount to his own businesses. Again, he was obliged to leave. By this time, however, he had begun to establish a personal fortune of his own, which came to include a hotel group in Singapore.

Khoo had also established a separate bank in Brunei, in 1965. Khoo was the only foreigner, apart from Enrique Zobel, who had been given permission to establish a bank in Brunei. This bank, the National Bank of Brunei, also grew very fast and became the bank with the most branches in the Sultanate.

The bank, like other prudent ventures in Brunei, included members of the royal family among its shareholders. While Khoo and other members of his family were thought to own 70 per cent or more, Prince Mohamed became president and a director of the bank. Then Prince Sufri succeeded him as President in 1984, when Prince Mohamed became Foreign Minister. The company registry in 1986 also showed Queen Saleha in the list of 277 shareholders. The Sultan himself was almost certainly a shareholder. The share capital and reserves of the bank at that time were shown as B$184 million (equivalent to £57.5 million).

Khoo's personal relationship with the Sultan may not have been that close. Khoo was seventy in 1987 and of the Sultan's father's generation. But Khoo knew the value of personal contact and sent his son, Khoo Ban Hock, on weekly trips to Brunei. Khoo Ban Hock was a well-padded, affable man who was popular and un-ambitious. He obediently went to Brunei every Thursday morning, visiting the National Bank and then going on to the Istana Nurul Iman, the largest palace. He would run errands for members of the royal family and bring such things as food, jewellery and computers from the cosmopolitan shops of Singapore. He also brought the latest gossip to entertain them.

As mentioned earlier, the Sultan used to stay in the flagship hotel of the Khoo family, the Goodwood Park Hotel. But the Sultan had decided he wanted a suite permanently available to him and he had bought from Tan Sri Khoo another of his hotels, the Singapore Holiday Inn. The Khoo family continued to sit on the board and effectively continued running the hotel. It was claimed by some that Tan Sri Khoo charged the Sultan too much for the sale of the Holiday Inn. But the Sultan did buy the hotel at a time when the hotel business in Singapore and Brunei was booming. If the Sultan failed to see the slump that was coming, that was not Khoo's fault. In any case, the Sultan clearly did not hold a grudge, since it was after the Holiday Inn deal that the Sultan conferred the honorary title of 'Datuk' on his son, the clubbable Khoo Ban Hock.

Tan Sri Khoo's wealth continued to grow and he did a major deal with one of the other foreign advisers of the Sultan. In 1981 he bought the Southern Pacific Hotel Corporation in Australia from Adnan Khashoggi for A$105 million. Southern Pacific was, and remains, a major hotel group which includes hotels under the 'Travelodge' name. (Khoo sold the chain in 1988 for A$540 million.)

In 1984–5, the financial power and profile of Tan Sri Khoo seemed to increase dramatically. Khoo started trying to buy Wheelock Marden, a major, long-established Hong Kong trading company. At around the same time he also entered into negotiations for a major stake in Hongkong Land, which owns the lion's share of the best property in Hong Kong and is therefore one of the most valuable property companies in the world. He sold his stake in Wheelock Marden to a counter-bidder for a profit of some HK$110 million (about £10 million). The attempt to buy Hongkong Land was unsuccessful.

Khoo turned his attention to London and snapped up just under 30 per cent of Exco, the owner of Astley and Pearce, one of the two biggest money-broking companies in the world. Exco also owned Wico, a British stockbroking company with a valuable seat on the Tokyo Stock Exchange. Another former Exco holding was a majority stake in Telerate, the American financial information company. This was sold in 1985 for US$460 million in cash.

Khoo then bought a 5 per cent stake in Standard and Chartered

Bank, a leading bank in the Far East and Africa. Standard Chartered also owned Union Bank Corporation in California and United Bank Corporation in Arizona. Meanwhile Khoo's less important share-dealing included purchases of minority stakes in two leading Singapore banks, the D B S Bank and the United Overseas Bank.

This was quite a spending spree for someone who previously invested relatively modest sums of money. The stake in Exco, for example, cost him £116.5 million for his initial 22 per cent block and then more, pro rata, for the rest of his holding. He still held that stake while also buying the Standard Chartered shares and the shares in the Singapore banks. As for Hongkong Land, it would have cost him over one billion pounds had he bought it at the price he was considering.

Khoo's suddenly stronger finances led to some speculation that the Sultan's money might be behind his efforts. It was noted that Khoo had obtained his stake in Exco from the Kuwaiti Investment Office, whose ultimate bosses might be expected to have a friendly attitude to a fellow Muslim leader such as the Sultan. Khoo denied categorically that the Sultan's money was backing him. But he made this denial from the comfort of the Sultan's London hotel, the Dorchester. This, he explained, was merely because he had not been able to get another hotel room in London and had got one at the Dorchester through his relationship with the Sultan. (Staff of the Dorchester were told by Khoo that his stays there had been approved by the Sultan. The staff tried to check this but, like others before and after, had difficulty in reaching the Sultan to confirm what Khoo had told them.)

The mystery over how Khoo had become such a splashy spender continued. We now know that in fact he was telling the truth when he said the Sultan's money was not behind him. Yes, Khoo had financed his deals in Brunei, but not through the Sultan. He had used his bank in Brunei to finance the deals. He had used his bank in a way that shows just what can be done if a bank is cleverly manipulated. His operations there were outrageous by international standards of banking. They were also outrageously successful in deceiving many a famous international bank.

What he did, in essence, was direct 90 per cent of the bank's lending to his own companies. His bank in Brunei became a means by which he borrowed vast sums of money without the lenders being aware of what was going on. He induced ordinary Bruneians and international banks alike to put their money into the National Bank of Brunei. He did this by making the bank look as though it had a sound capital base that was being built up year after year by increasing profits. This was a fiction perpetrated by false accounting.

The only way in which the National Bank, or any bank, could show profits was by appearing to receive interest on the loans it had made. But Khoo's companies were not, in many cases, paying interest at all. The interest due on their loans was simply added to the total amount due.

Another trick for boosting profits was the omission from the profit-and-loss account of some of the interest payments made by the bank to depositors. This was done by balancing the interest payments with some fictional new debts owed to the bank.

But artificially boosted profits were not enough. Khoo needed the appearance of growth in ordinary deposits and loans at the bank to help convince overseas bankers that the bank was a worthy recipient of large inter-bank loans. The trick was worked by the National Bank lending money to a Khoo company, which sent it to a second Khoo company, which in turn deposited it back with the National Bank. Thus, in appearance, the bank had extra deposits and loans. In fact, it was all on paper and meant nothing.

More than thirty foreign banks were taken in by these devices, including American Express Bank, Swiss Bank Corporation and Standard Chartered Bank. The money was not, as they expected, used to expand the National Bank's business in Brunei. It was sent directly to Khoo companies in Singapore and Hong Kong and used to acquire the stakes in companies like Wheelock Marden, Exco and Standard Chartered. Swiss Bank Corporation, for example, granted a £20.8 million loan in February 1986 for the purchase of shares in Exco.

Khoo also borrowed in his own name. In July 1986 American Express Bank agreed to lend US$100 million directly to Khoo for the purpose of buying shares in Standard Chartered Bank. American Express was content to lend Khoo 85 per cent of the value of the

Standard Chartered shares he bought. But the point was that Khoo could borrow much more by adding to his own creditworthiness the creditworthiness of the National Bank.

This deception of other banks might have continued for many more years but for the belated attempts of the Brunei government to bring itself up-to-date in regulating banks. In early 1986 the Brunei Finance Ministry sent several officials to the United States for training as bank examiners. This development was very probably influenced by the presence of an American, Ted Smith, who had been employed by the Finance Ministry and became one of its most trusted advisers. (If so, that would mean that this American guest in the Far East was responsible for the downfall of one of the most long-established tycoons there.)

In July 1986, freshly back from their training, the examiners examined the new financial data that was now required monthly from the banks and found that National Bank was borrowing money from abroad. This was the opposite of what the other banks did. All the others generated excess funds in Brunei which they then deposited abroad.

Later the same month, on 25 July, the examiners learned that this borrowing abroad was going to be carried a stage further. National Bank was going to float US$30 million of floating-rate notes through a Swiss bank called Banque Gutzwiller Kurz Bungener, based in Geneva. The newly trained examiners demanded explanations and details from National Bank. This is how they began to discover that 90 per cent of the loans of the National Bank were to Khoo's own companies. Local loans were only B$99 million whereas total loans, including those to Khoo companies, were B$1.47 billion, equivalent at that time to about US$687 million.

Though scandalized by what had happened, the Bruneian authorities nevertheless were willing to negotiate with Tan Sri Khoo over how and when he might provide collateral or else repay the loans. But the patience of the Bruneian authorities wore thin and in November 1986 they laid charges against his son, Khoo Ban Hock, and other officers of the bank. A British accountant, Andrew Peattie, was also charged. Altogether charges were laid against six people. Negotiations still continued after these criminal charges were brought, but a settlement was not reached before the cases came to court.

The trial, which began in October 1987, was a bizarre event. Much of the talk was between a British judge, a British Queen's Counsel prosecuting and another British Queen's Counsel defending Khoo Ban Hock. The proceedings were like those in the law courts in the Strand, central London. Yet when one stepped outside, there was the blazing sunlight of the tropics. The British lawyers who had to stay in the Sheraton-Utama Hotel became monumentally bored with life in Brunei, consoling themselves only with the thought of what fat fees they were earning. A couple of lawyers together with a journalist covering the case found that the only way to relieve the tedium one night was to quiz each other in the hotel bar on obscure details of the case. Every time one of them failed to answer a question, he or she had to drink a glass of champagne. In this fashion, the three of them drank five bottles of champagne, which cost B$404 (US$202). Whether or not the cost found its way into a lawyer's expense account is unknown.

The only other amusement at the time was provided by the fate of one of the defendants who was allowed to leave Brunei when the prosecution decided not to proceed with the charges against him. He picked up his aeroplane ticket and headed for the airport, but when he got to immigration, the officials queried his departure. In a classic example of Brunei bureaucracy at work, the man who had been forcibly kept in jail for four months and had then been prohibited by the court from leaving Brunei for another four months was told he could not leave because his visa had expired. (Eventually, the confusion was sorted out and the man was allowed to go.)

While those attending the case were bored, the accused found jail a dreadful experience. The man who was released, Chiew Sung Ching, said his jail cell was small and his bed was a concrete slab with straw matting. He found his time in jail traumatic and he said later, 'I've changed. I wouldn't even kill the cockroaches and the flies that came into my cell. I helped them to get out through the hole.' Khoo Ban Hock lost at least a stone of weight and looked a shadow of his former plump self.

In December 1987 Khoo Ban Hock and another defendant

changed their pleas. They admitted guilt to some of the charges while, simultaneously, others were dropped. The next month Andrew Peattie, the British accountant, followed suit. It seemed that a compromise had been reached between the prosecution and the defence. So at last the British lawyers could go home, while their clients served out the remainder of relatively modest sentences. Khoo Ban Hock received by far the longest sentence, and that was only four years and four months. Even that was reduced on appeal to three years. Only three out of the original six charged were sentenced at all. The point was that the big fish was not in the tank. Tan Sri Khoo had been the brains behind the National Bank and he was not in Brunei. In fact, he was nowhere to be found at all. He was avoiding all risk of being extradited to Brunei.

The irony of the whole episode was that Khoo probably did not have any intention of defrauding anyone at all. Yes, his assistants were found guilty of conspiring to defraud and false accounting, but almost certainly it was Khoo's intention to repay the loans which he obtained via the National Bank.

Nevertheless, the fact remains that Khoo had taken advantage of the Brunei royal family and their naivety in financial affairs. He had seduced them with trinkets while using a bank in their country to deceive international banks worldwide. Khoo had ultimately brought yet more embarrassment to Brunei. After the Sultan had already borne the criticisms over Zobel's palace, the ugly controversy over Al-Fayed's purchase of House of Fraser and the humbling arrest of the Swami, such further embarrassment could not be welcome. It was hard to avoid concluding that the Sultan had made another mistake in his choice of whom to trust. The Sultan was also disillusioned by another person he thought he could trust. The only compensation in this separate incident was that on this occasion the matter did not, until now, come to the notice of the media.

The following incident took place in 1986. It overlaps the story of Khoo but is completely unconnected. It certainly includes in its elements conspiracy and corruption, but while the Khoo story is now relatively clear, having been held up to view in court, this second story remains very mysterious. Obtaining information on it is all but impossible. Those most closely involved are the Brunei government, which will say nothing, General Ver of the Philippines, who is in hiding, and the former Grand Chamberlain of Brunei, a brother-in-law of the Sultan, who is thought to be in jail if he is not dead.

The background to the incident is the revolution in the Philippines which in February 1986 saw the removal of the discredited President Ferdinand Marcos and his replacement by President Corazon Aquino. Among the loyal supporters of President Marcos before the revolution was the bald, ambitious General Ver, Chief of Staff of the army at the time when the former leader of the opposition to Marcos, Benigno Aquino, was murdered at Manila airport. Ver was, as a result of this coincidence of facts, unpopular in the Philippines. Marcos removed him from his position in the army prior to the elections of 1986 in an attempt to court popularity for himself. General Ver nevertheless retained great influence in the army because so many officers were loyal to him personally.

General Ver had a lifestyle which reflected wealth considerably larger than that which could easily be afforded on a soldier's salary. He showered his mistress, Edna Camcam, with luxury presents and had a fleet of Mercedes cars.

Marcos claimed that he won the election, but he eventually succumbed to the pressure of the crowd and the encouragement of the United States to leave the Philippines in a hurry. With him on the departing flight was General Ver.

Under the new regime, the General's fleet of Mercedes cars was sequestered and he was cited as a principal in renewed proceedings concerning the murder of Benigno Aquino. He has not made himself available for interview by the new government of the Philippines. He did, however, appear in a court hearing in Virginia, in the United States, concerning the misdirection of United States aid to the Philippines during the Marcos years.

After General Ver left the Philippines with Marcos, he often travelled incognito. He was once sighted in Singapore wearing a wig, doubtless hoping that it would be a good disguise, since he is bald. But too many Filipinos visit Singapore and he is too famous or infamous to be able to walk the streets there for long without being recognized. He was also sighted in Brunei and it is there that he appears to have been involved in a conspiracy with the Grand Chamberlain, Pengiran Tahiruddin, the husband of one of the Sultan's sisters. Another person allegedly involved was Dato Marsal, the son of a former chief minister of Brunei. Clearly General Ver had obtained the cooperation of some of the top people in Brunei.

The nature of the conspiracy is not certain. There appears to have been drug-smuggling into Brunei. There is also a report from well-placed sources that they were also dealing in arms and women. The purpose of the smuggling and dealing certainly seems to have been directed in part at least towards making money. Another widely canvassed possibility is that they were laundering money previously obtained in the Philippines. Pengiran Tahiruddin made enquiries at that time about investing in a casino on Christmas Island which could have cost hundreds of millions of Brunei dollars (well over a US$100 million).

But the dealing in arms indicates that more was involved than only money-making. It seems quite likely that General Ver was involved in trying to support a counter-revolution in the Philippines. The first two years of the new Aquino government saw five coup attempts. Many army officers still supported the previous regime. It would be surprising if General Ver had not been in contact with some of them, offering encouragement and material support.

The most extreme story concerning General Ver's activities in Brunei is that he and Pengiran Tahiruddin were plotting assassinations. According to this story, General Ver was recruiting Philippine workers who would come to Brunei to work on construction projects there. They would be supplied with money and arms, then, when President Aquino visited Brunei later in 1986, Pengiran Tahiruddin, using his trusted position as Grand Chamberlain, would let these worker/terrorists into the dining room at a state banquet where they would assassinate President Aquino. Then General Ver would lead a counter-revolution in the Philippines. Meanwhile the Grand Chamberlain, having arranged the death of the Sultan too, would make himself or some member of the royal family the new Sultan.

This bizarre story does have the circumstantial support that President Aquino was due to visit Brunei in 1986 and that the visit was postponed.

The conspiracies of General Ver and Pengiran Tahiruddin, whatever they were, came to an abrupt end. The how and why of it has, once again, not been announced or confirmed. But it is widely believed in Brunei that it happened like this: On 19 August, Lee Kuan Yew, the Prime Minister of Singapore, visited Brunei in person, accompanied by, among others, his Minister of Law. Naturally he had a private meeting with the Sultan, and it is thought that he informed the Sultan that officials at Singapore airport had detected illegal goods in transit to Brunei and ultimately destined for General Ver and/or Tahiruddin. (Whether these goods were arms or drugs is uncertain.) The smugglers had tried to make the passage of the goods easier by using the Sultan's name.

Again there is circumstantial evidence to support this story. Within days of Lee Kuan Yew's visit to Brunei, Pengiran Tahiruddin and members of his family were arrested. It is thought that Dato Marsal was also arrested. The fate of Tahiruddin and Marsal is not clear at all. They do not appear to have faced any public trial, but they certainly have disappeared from view. It is believed that they are in jail if they are not dead. Amnesty International has been unable to ascertain whether they are being held without trial, but that seems to be very likely. It may well be that they deserve to be in jail, but they have not yet had a chance to defend themselves.

As for General Ver, he slipped away. His mistress, Edna Camcam, is thought to be in Britain, and the Philippines intelligence service believes that General Ver visits her. Ver is believed by the Philippines government to have travelled on a forged passport bearing the name of his son-in-law, Victor Tuazon. He is also thought to have travelled on a Colombian passport issued by an honorary consul for Colombia in the Philippines. The Philippines Embassy in London has asked the British government to discover whether Ver has come to Britain on the Colombian passport. At the time of writing, the government has not given a reply. Where General Ver is living now is anyone's guess.

Chicanery, conspiracy, corruption and mystery. These seem to be often drawn to the Sultan. His money, and the way he is willing to spend it, attracts unconventional high-flyers, particularly in politics and finance. Yet many of these high-flyers who involve themselves in Brunei seem to end up in difficulties. Tan Sri Khoo and General Ver have now been added to the list. Next comes Colonel Oliver North.

CHAPTER EIGHTEEN

Cheque-Book Diplomacy

——————— ☙ ———————

We greatly appreciate your support for this endeavour, which we believe has great importance for the overall security of the free world.

George Shultz, Secretary of State for Foreign Affairs, in a letter to the Sultan of Brunei, 1986

The Sultan's brother, Prince Mohamed, is Foreign Minister of Brunei. But whenever there is a starring role to be had in foreign affairs, Sultan Hassanal is on stage himself.

To his credit, the Sultan has certainly kept a wary eye on the strategic defence interests of Brunei. Whatever misfortunes may have dogged his foreign policies, these policies have at least been consistently aimed at pacifying those who might conceivably attack him and confirming friendships with those who might conceivably defend him. In particular, he has sought to cement Brunei's place in the Association of South-East Asian Nations, which admitted Brunei as a member in 1984. This association is theoretically about economics, but in practice it is also an unofficial mutual-security pact among six South-East Asian nations. The Sultan does not lack a sense of where his safety lies.

His basic common sense, though, is not enough to make him look good at the international meetings he attends. The Sultan usually seems tense, like a schoolboy who has been spruced up to meet friends of his parents. He is dressed immaculately in silk suits that look as though they are being worn for the first time. He dresses more sharply than most of the politicians he meets – he even wears ankle-high boots. His speeches give every sign of being written by a bureaucrat who dares not stray from restating what had been said before. One of the statements ritually repeated is condemnation of South African apartheid. This stance is common in the worldwide Muslim community and that, perhaps, is why Brunei has adopted it. But the stance is particularly awkward for a country which itself practises racial discrimination.

But anyway, the Sultan's mind at international meetings does not always focus on politics. In fact one of his main concerns at the Commonwealth Heads of Government Meeting in Vancouver in 1987 was to fly himself in his own Gulfstream aeroplane to the country retreat to which all the heads of government were going for more informal meetings. The Canadian authorities had great difficulty persuading him that he should go in the same transport as that provided for other world leaders.

The Sultan's early experience of diplomacy was quite successful. By the late 1970s relations with Malaysia had been strained for many years, not least because Malaysia had encouraged and supported rebels in Brunei and had even sent some for training in Libya. But by this time the Malaysians had decided that the chances of a successful democratic revolt in Brunei were remote. The time was ripe for the Sultan to patch things up.

Polo happens to be popular with several of the Sultans of Malaysian states. These Sultans have nothing approaching the power of the Sultan of Brunei (being part of a democratic country), but they have certain vestiges of authority and some of them are extremely wealthy.

The Sultan's best friends in the region became the polo playing royal families of Pahang and Johore. In the course of his 'polo diplomacy', the Sultan played with teams from both of these states. The royal families visited each other's countries. There was even talk of a marriage to cement the link between the families of Johore and Brunei.

The Sultan Mahmood Iskandar of Johore is currently taking his turn as King (Agong) of Malaysia. His status is therefore as close as it could be to that of the Sultan. This present King of Malaysia has what one local paper discreetly described as 'a boisterous and chequered career studded with a few brushes with the law'. These 'few brushes' include admitted culpable homicide. His son, the Prince Regent of Johore, gets on particularly well with the Sultan.

Also close are the Sultan's relations with the Pahang royal family. The Sultan of Pahang is a keen sportsman and some younger members of his family are known to be as fun-loving as the Sultan of Brunei himself and his brother Prince Jefri. The Pahang family has a beautiful palace with a polo ground in front of it and a golf course around it.

Through his contacts with these families, the Sultan broke the ice in relations with Malaysia. However, it seems with hindsight like beginner's luck.

In 1984, the Sultan moved on to the international stage through the independence of Brunei. He attempted to make an impact in the United States and Britain. In Britain he may have received some guidance from Mohammed Al-Fayed. His main diplomatic tactic seemed to be the issuing of cheques. He gave money to several charities in Britain, including the National Army Museum. The donations amounted to some £3 million, but they were made discreetly. When the Sultan visited New York to join the United Nations formally, he donated US$1 million to the UN Children's Fund. He also surprised Mayor Ed Koch by handing over a cheque for US$500,000 for the homebound elderly of New York. This was done very publicly and doubtless seemed like a good public-relations move at the time. In return the mayor gave him the key to the city. But back home in Brunei, these donations were not such a success. Some people felt that the Sultan should not be giving away Brunei's wealth to people thousands of miles away when there were still poor people in Brunei itself.

After that, the Sultan's gifts became either secret (as in the case of the major donation we are coming to) or else more heavily covered with a cloak of international diplomacy. The Sultan lent US$100 million to Indonesian projects, half of which went to help the financing of a proposed toll road. The terms of the loans caused some confusion. According to one report, the Sultan wanted an interest rate even lower than the Indonesians had sought. In any case, the interest rate was either nominal or zero and repayment was not to be due for a quarter of a century. These doughnut-soft loans did not give offence at home because they were loans, not gifts, and they appeared to foster good relations with the most powerful neighbouring country. The Sultan's tendency to treat other nations as private fiefdoms like his own was reflected in the fact that the loan benefited business associates of the Indonesian president.

In the mid-1980s the Sultan developed friendly relations with several Middle Eastern states such as Oman, which shared the same religion and also enjoyed wealth derived from energy reserves. The closest of these relationships was with Jordan.

The introduction was probably established by the Pahang royal family. This family had played polo with a team from Jordan for some years, and the Sultan of Pahang arranged for the Jordanian polo team (which is closely connected to the Jordanian royal family) to come to play at the Sultan of Brunei's international tournament. The Sultan and King Hussein of Jordan found that they have plenty in common. They both rule by virtue of their royal blood rather than an electoral mandate. They both are Sunni Muslims. They are both engaged in restraining religious fundamentalists in their own country. Each has a long-standing association with Britain. They had both gone to Sandhurst, they both have contact with the British royal family and they both have houses in Britain. Their wives created another link. Both the Sultan and the King had married women with foreign blood. In King Hussein's case, his wife is American.

The Jordanians took over the running of the Sultan's private fleet of aeroplanes. These planes used to be run by the highly regarded West German airline Lufthansa. But early in 1986 the Sultan sacked Lufthansa and replaced them with Jordanian aircrew. Various stories circulated in Brunei about the reasons for the switch, but none could be confirmed. What was certainly true was that the Sultan's fleet of planes was suddenly militarized. The collective name for the Sultan's planes was changed from the Royal Flight (a phrase taken from the British royal family's aeroplanes) to the Royal Squadron (the phrase used for King Hussein's planes).

The men who crewed the Jordanian royal squadron and the Brunei Royal Squadron were trained for flying jet fighters. Jordan is particularly proud of its airforce and boasts that Jordan is the only Middle Eastern country to have shot down Israeli jets in aerial dog fights. Jordan has Western equipment and has already helped to train Iraq to use such equipment.

Jordan was doubtless well paid by Brunei for its aeroplane services and Jordan expected to sell other services too in fields like civil engineering, medicine and construction. It seemed like the beginning of a long-term alliance of Muslim monarchies. Brunei provided the money and Jordan the experience and expertise. But this friendship ended as quickly as it had begun, and more mysteriously. Suddenly the Jordanian aircrews were told to go. King Hussein, it seems, was keen that they should leave in a Royal Jordanian aeroplane rather than suffer the indignity of being shipped out on a Bruneian flight. So the King diverted a Royal Jordanian flight to take them out.

Why were the Jordanians sacked? There are stories in Brunei that concern Prince Jefri, who among other things is head of Royal Brunei Airlines. There are also stories that involve one or more of the attractive air hostesses employed by Royal Jordanian. These air hostesses included at that time an Irish woman and a Spanish woman. The Spaniard was of an appearance that dazed-looking expatriates described as 'stunning'. However, whether they really played any part in the ending of the Jordanian contract is utterly unknown.

Lufthansa regained its original position. The episode seemed farcical. But when it comes to farce in Bruneian foreign policy, this was not the high point by a long way.

In August 1986 a representative of the Sultan arranged to meet a 'Mr Kenilworth' in a hotel near Hyde Park. 'Mr Kenilworth' was not his real name, but was a false name suggested by the Sultan's representative, who was concerned that their telephone conversations were being bugged. Perhaps he was also concerned that conversations in his hotel room would similarly be bugged, since they left the hotel and walked out into Hyde Park to have a secret conversation among the trees and flowers.

'Mr Kenilworth' was an American. He asked for US$10 million. The money was not for himself. Nor was the money for the American government, of which he was a senior member. The money was for the 'rebels' or 'freedom fighters' battling against the government of Nicaragua – the Contras. For the Sultan, the sum of US$10 million was not very significant. But as the two men wandered between the green trees of London's best-known park, the Sultan's representative asked 'Mr Kenilworth', 'What do we get out of this? What's in it for us?'

'Mr Kenilworth', really Assistant Secretary of State Elliott Abrams, replied, 'You will have the gratitude of the Secretary [of State] and the President.'

The Sultan's man could not give an immediate 'yes' or 'no'; he would have to confer. But the Sultan quickly made a decision to pay over the money that would buy the gratitude of the President of the United States, no less. Good relations with the United States' administration was part of Brunei's natural foreign-policy strategy. A condition of the gift was that it should remain a secret.

The Sultan's favourable decision was communicated to the American State Department and the Sultan received in reply a private note of gratitude from the Secretary of State, George Shultz. 'We greatly appreciate your support for this endeavour,' wrote Shultz, 'which we believe has great importance for the overall security of the free world.'

The Sultan must have felt very pleased with this personal venture into high diplomacy. Not least among the benefits were that during 1986, both before and after his donation, he received unprecedented attention from the United States. In June 1986 he was visited by George Shultz in person. In September of the same year he was invited to visit the United States aircraft-carrier *Carl Vinson*. He was forced to cancel this visit because of his father's death, but the United States offered another aircraft-carrier, the *Kitty Hawk*, and another visit, which took place in January 1987. The Americans later denied that this hospitality had anything to do with the Sultan's Contra donation, but clearly Brunei had become a favoured friend of the United States' administration.

Back in Washington, Elliott Abrams visited the office of Lieutenant-Colonel Oliver North, who was spearheading the US administration's supply of unofficial aid to the Contras. Abrams asked North (who was doubtless delighted that the Sultan was willing to contribute so much to the Contra cause) for the name and number of the account to which the Sultan should send his money. Originally the money was going to be sent to an account in the Bahamas, but North gave him a note of a different account number, that of Lake Resources Inc. at Crédit Suisse, 11 Rue Versonnex, Eaux-Vives, Geneva, Switzerland. Curiously, this branch of Crédit Suisse is not the main branch in Geneva – a massive building in the centre of the business district. Eaux-Vives is a more modest part of town on the east side, just south of Lake Leman. Hence, perhaps, the name of the account, 'Lake Resources'.

North's secretary, Fawn Hall, typed out the account number for Abrams on a card. Abrams took the card and sent out the details to the Sultan. The account number he sent was 368 430 221. The Sultan accordingly instructed the National Bank of Brunei (which was not yet in disgrace) to effect payment. The money was transferred from an account at Citibank in Zurich to the Crédit Suisse account in Geneva.

But the number of the account given to the Sultan was wrong. The correct number of the Lake Resources Inc. account was 386 430 221, not 368 430 221. Somehow, someone in Washington had transposed two of the digits. The number given to the Sultan and to which the money was sent was not the account of Lake Resources at all; it was the account of a sixty-year-old Swiss shipping magnate. Officials at the Eaux-Vives branch of Crédit Suisse were probably a little surprised that the money should be credited to that particular account at all, which was inactive. However, the money was credited to the account and the shipping magnate was duly notified.

The magnate, delighted no doubt, quickly removed the money from his inactive account at Crédit Suisse and placed it instead at another bank in Geneva: Banque Paribas (Suisse) S A at 2 Place de Hollande. The magnate bought a certificate of deposit there which proceeded to earn him interest.

Elliott Abrams, meanwhile, was somewhat concerned about the failure of the U S$10 million to arrive. Several times he asked Oliver North whether the money had come. Each time he was told it had not. For three months Abrams and North patiently waited. They would have raised an alarm had they realized the money had been sent. Presumably they did not know. The Sultan therefore must have sent the US$10 million without simultaneously sending notification to Abrams that he had done so. In other words, he must have sent US$10 million without telling the intended recipients what he was doing and without checking that the money had arrived. Thus, nobody realized that the money had gone astray.

Three months later, in November 1986, the Iran–Contra scandal began to break. Abrams decided that it would be better now if the Sultan did not send the money after all. So he sent a telex to the United States Embassy in Brunei, which is in a small block of offices in the main street of the capital. A diplomat in Brunei telexed back that a Brunei official was 'visibly shaken' when told that the US$10 million had not been received in the Lake Resources account.

The United States authorities asked for the help of the Swiss government in tracing the money on 12 December. But progress was very slow until the end of April 1987, when the Senate Committee investigating the Iran–Contra affair asked for assistance from the New York branch of Crédit Suisse. The Senate Committee obtained authorization from the Sultan to act on his behalf in locating the money and a committee accountant went to Switzerland in early May. Within days, on 7 May 1987, Crédit Suisse lodged a 'complaint' against the Swiss magnate who had received the US$10 million in error. The magnate claimed that he had been expecting an amount of that sort and had accepted the money in good faith.

The money was quickly frozen and then released back to the Sultan. Brunei officials then let it be known that the Sultan had intended the money for 'humanitarian aid' in Central America. It was an ineffective way to reduce the Sultan's embarrassment. True, the Sultan did not have to face the kind of questioning a democratic leader would have met. He did not have to explain why he thought humanitarian aid was needed in Central America more than elsewhere or why he had demanded a pledge from the United States government that the aid should be kept secret. Humanitarian aid is something most heads of state do not keep secret. But the story of his botched attempt to hand over money for a cause that even many United States congressmen consider dubious did nothing for the Sultan's reputation.

The US government had not had any intention of fulfilling any promise, if it was made, to spend all the US$10 million on 'humanitarian' aid. According to one witness, Albert Hakim, at the Senate Committee investigation, Richard V. Secord intended to allocate US$3 million, at the very least, to weapons for the Contras.

Thus did the Sultan's best-known foreign policy initiative come to an embarrassing end. The attempted gift had been a pathetic cloak-and-dagger farce. The gift was probably a bad idea in the first place. But the bad idea was badly executed and then exposed. It was the worst possible outcome.

But more embarrassment was to come. This received less publicity, although it was potentially a more dangerous incident for Brunei. In 1987, the Malaysian Prime Minister, Datuk Seri Mahathir Mohamed, visited Brunei and had a meeting with the Sultan. The *Far Eastern Economic Review* reported that the two men had discussed the possible sale of Limbang, some Malaysian territory, to Brunei. Limbang is a wedge of land which divides Brunei in two and which Brunei has long claimed as its own. The magazine report was damaging to Prime Minister Mahathir because his rivals could portray the alleged incident as showing that Mahathir was willing to sell his own country. Mahathir denied that any such negotiations had taken place and sued the *Far Eastern Economic Review*.

The Sultan, who might have settled the issue, was, not for the first time, uncommunicative. He never denied or confirmed that Limbang was discussed. This was hardly likely to endear him to the Malaysian Prime Minister. However opponents of Mahathir could only derive satisfaction from the Sultan's silence. These opponents included Tunku Razaleigh Hamzah, who was of royal blood and who was friendly with the Sultan's brother, Prince Jefri. The Sultan appeared to be playing with fire by, inadvertently perhaps, getting involved in the very heart of Malaysia's political power struggles. The danger was especially great because of the fact that Brunei is surrounded by Malaysian territory except on its seashore.

Few admire the diplomacy of Brunei. Indeed, the hardworking meritocrats of Singapore are sometimes infuriated to see their relaxed Bruneian counterparts taking things easy and drawing bigger salaries. Brunei's foreign policy has been marked by blunders and embarrassments of which the Contra incident is the most famous. But at least there have been no serious consequences. The Sultan has been lucky. The days of invasions in South-East Asia seem to have passed. He knows whom he must not anger too much and it would take a very big blunder now for his rule to be endangered by a foreign country.

Indeed, is there any danger to his rule at all?

CHAPTER NINETEEN

Conclusion

A great fortune is a great slavery.
>Seneca, *Ad Polybium de Consolatione*, first century A D

The fact that the Bruneian monarchy has survived as long as it has is a remarkable fluke. The monarchy managed to continue during the years of British 'protection' only because the Sultan was useful to the British. He was a symbol of local status and tradition. It may seem cynical to say so, but the Sultan in those years appeared to become a tool with which the British fended off various threats while a part-British company, Shell, extracted the oil and gas.

The royal family was fortunate that British self-interest coincided with its own and that the kukri knives of the British-employed Gurkhas were unsheathed to cut down the country's 1962 rebellion. The present Sultan was also fortunate that by the time he took up the reins of power in the mid-1980s, the major post-war movements towards socialism, Communism and democracy had all slowed down or even gone into reverse. His father and the British had seen off the crisis years. But crisis years will surely return.

It was one thing for the Sultans of the past to be held in awe by the poor and uneducated. But the rich, well-travelled, well-educated elite that is quickly developing in Brunei will not be content to bow and scrape to an absolute monarch forever. Democracy in South-East Asia has had its reverses in recent years, but its spirit is still alive and kicking, as the Philippines, Taiwan and South Korea have demonstrated.

The absolute rule of the Sultan's family cannot last forever. Either the royal family will accept a constitutional role within a democracy or else it will be toppled by a coup or revolt. Dynastic rule is extremely vulnerable anywhere in the world, and that includes East and South-East Asia. The monarchies that have survived in the region tend, like the monarchies of Malaysia, Thailand and Japan, to have accepted a constitutional role. The royal family of Brunei is not so impressive that it can expect to be an exception for very long.

For the time being, the Sultanate is calmer than ever. The Sultan has his defences. He has armed himself with Islamic rectitude and Bruneian tradition. He has become increasingly aware of what he has to do to hold on to the throne. He attends the major ceremonies, he shows respect for Islam and he holds the strategic high points of power. The Sultan himself is Minister of Defence and doubtless also has direct control of the secret service. On top of that he can probably rely on the British-controlled Gurkhas. He also has his own regiment of retired Gurkhas, who are effectively his Praetorian Guard. In fact, his rule is probably best understood by reference to the Roman Empire in its decline. Intrigue and vice are not un-common among the elite in Brunei, just as they were not in Rome. Instead of consulting oracles, the leaders consult bomohs and as-trologers. Instead of whiling away their leisure hours watching gladiators and lions, they play polo and golf. The regime is past its prime and too much concerned with self-indulgence for its own good, just as Rome was after Augustus. But the Sultan's rule is well-enough established to continue for a good while yet.

The royal family of Brunei may gradually decline at the top in the same way that the Roman Imperial family did. Brunei could be regarded as a massive experiment in spoiling children. The Sultan's son by Mariam, Prince Azim, was at first a sparkling testimonial to the virtue of cross-breeding, but he is now said to be given so much attention and privilege that it is going to his head. The next genera-tion is going to have had an upbringing clothed in Yves St Laurent and smothered in Chanel No. 5. They may not go so far as to produce a Caligula or a Nero, but the line may well decay and there is plenty of scope for renewal of strife within the royal family. As for the present Sultan, he was probably brought up with sufficient discipline to see him through. His early years were not lived in luxury at all. His time in the Victorian Institution and Sandhurst gave him some sense of proportion and order.

One of the first questions asked in this book was whether or not the Sultan has been brought happiness by his wealth. Lethal traps are placed along his apparently easy path of power and wealth. There is the temptation for him always to spend his way out of his problems, to indulge himself out of depression and to listen to those who offer subtle flattery instead of blunt truth. The traps of being effortlessly wealthy have been so deftly side-stepped by most of the British royal family that it is hard for people in Britain in particular to realize how difficult they are to avoid. The Sultan has sometimes been ensnared. Sometimes his vanity has led him to trust those he should not have trusted.

Yet the Sultan's lot certainly does not invite pity. The luxury of the Sultan's life has been extensively described here. Details have been given of his houses and hotels all over the world; the sports and games he plays; the casinos and night-clubs he has visited; the planes, jacuzzis, gyms, swimming pools, polo ponies, golf courses, tennis courts and squash courts that he owns. He has two wives, many children and ostensibly plenty of friends. He is welcomed wherever he goes and treated with respect.

Yet his association with the bizarre and dubious Indian spiritual teacher, the Swami, and other spiritual guides shows that his mind has not been at ease. His main objective in life, to the extent that he has one, is to hold on to his position of power. Even this purpose has no meaning of which he can be proud. It represents only the denial to his fellow Bruneians of the democratic control which they have previously shown they would prefer. And the self-discipline he must show to hold on to his power must be a persistent strain.

He does not rule particularly well, so he is also denied the satisfaction that achievement would bring. Sports and games take up much of his time, but they, too, surely do not create a meaning for his life. He probably devotes so much time to them because he is bored.

Being the richest man in the world affords the Sultan many privileges, thrills and luxuries, but happiness, surely, is not one of them. He has everything he could want in the material world, but when it comes to the things that really matter, he is no richer than you or I.

The Sultan's wealth is a phenomenon that intrigues because it is so extreme. But his wealth is dependent on absolute political power. Such power in the hands of one man is becoming increasingly rare and his family will surely not manage to keep it a great deal longer. We may not see his like again.

Index

Index

Index

Nabila (yacht), 30–31, 140, 156, 169
Nandy, Pritish, 136–7
National Bank of Brunei, 171–7
National Army Museum, 184
night clubs, 23–6
Noorhayati, Princess (wife of Prince Jefri), 56, 90, 113
North, Colonel Oliver, 187–8

Observer newspaper, 144, 147–9, 153, 157, 161–2
oil industry, development of, see also Shell, 6, 13–15, 19
Omar Ali Saifuddien, Sultan, 4, 6–7, 10, 53, 65–76

Peattie, Andrew, 175, 177
polo, 29, 36–42, 65, 123, 139, 183–4
polygamy, 65–6

QAF Holdings, 126–7, 160

Rajaratnam, Ponniah, 127–9, 161–2
Rashidah, Princess, 44
Reddy, Dr Prathap, 161
Rewald, Ronald, 43
Riachy, Charles, 24, 154, 164
Ritz Hotel (Paris), 140, 143, 147, 148, 158
Rowland, Roland 'Tiny', 144–56
Royal Dutch/Shell, see Shell
Royal Holiday Inn (Singapore), 95, 115, 161

Saleha, Queen (wife of Sultan), 10, 51, 54, 61, 73, 77–8, 171
Sandhurst, RMA, 10, 87, 194

Sears Holdings, 163
Seri Begawan, see Omar, Sultan
Shell (oil company), 13–14, 118, 121, 124, 134, 192
Shultz, George, 182, 187
Singh, Zail, 168
Smith, Ted, 175
Special Air Service (SAS), 86
Sufri, Prince, 58–9, 76, 171
Sunday Telegraph, 146, 148–9
'Swami' (Shri Chaudra Swamiji Maharaj), 134–7, 156–63, 167–9, 194

Tahiruddin, Pengiran, 178–80
television in Brunei, 83–4
Thatcher, Margaret, 139, 149, 154, 159
Thatcher, Mark, 149, 167
Travers-Clarke, Peter, 90
Turnbull and Asser, 163

UN Children's Fund, 184

Ventti, Geno, 90
Ver, General, 178–80
Victorian Institution, 8–10, 44, 194
Vincci shops, 34–5

Wadood, Pengiran, 70
Wales, Charles, Prince of, 2, 38, 69, 82, 111, 139, 163
Wardley (merchant bank), 20–21
Westbrook, Roger, 119

Zariah, Pengiran Anak, Princess, 54, 127
Zobel, Enrique, 41–52, 151, 158–61, 164, 169, 171